D0579765

decorating kids' rooms

from baby to teen

Mary Wynn Ryan
with Heidi Tyline King

Publications International, Ltd.

Mary Wynn Ryan is the author of Publications International's *The Ultimate Kitchen, The Ultimate Bath, Cottage Style, Fresh Country Style,* and *Garden Style* and has written about home furnishings and interior design for various magazines. She served as Midwest editor of *Design Times* magazine and was the director of consumer and trade marketing for the Chicago Merchandise Mart's residential design center. She is president of Winning Ways Marketing, an editorial and marketing consulting firm that specializes in home design and decorating.

Heidi Tyline King (crafts and home projects writer) is the author of *All About Paint and Wallpaper* and *Beautiful Wedding Crafts* and has contributed to *Easy Decorating* and *Family Fun Crafts.* Her articles on crafts, decorating, and home improvement have appeared in *Family Fun, Woman's Day,* and other national magazines.

Illustrator: Julie Ecklund

Copyright © 2003 Publications International, Ltd. All rights reserved. This book may not be reproduced or quoted in whole or in part by any means whatsoever without written permission from:

Louis Weber, CEO
Publications International, Ltd.
7373 North Cicero Avenue
Lincolnwood, Illinois 60712

Permission is never granted for commercial purposes.

Manufactured in China.

8 7 6 5 4 3 2 1

ISBN: 0-7853-6471-4

Library of Congress Control Number: 2002117338

Contents

Creating a Plan for Your Child's Room

Few tasks can be as delightful—and as daunting—as creating a room for that miraculous creature, your child. Since you're reading this book, it's clear your child's happiness and healthy development are high on your list of priorities. Whether you are decorating and furnishing your firstborn's room or are making a special place for later arrivals of any age, you know every child is a magical, unique individual who's constantly evolving. And no matter what your budget, you want your child's room to be as wonderful as he or she is. Relax. This book can help.

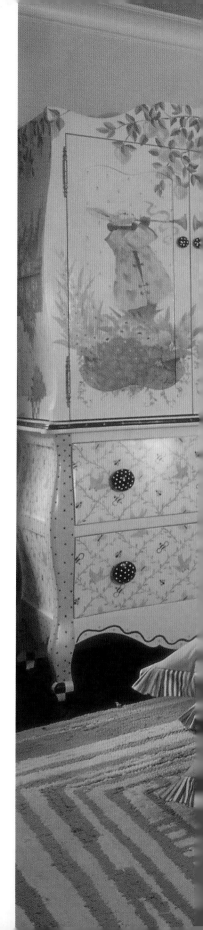

Whether you choose a fairy-tale theme or design a room around your child's favorite colors, coming up with a plan before you start buying things will create visual order and, ultimately, a space you and your child can be proud of. Designer: Julia Blailock, ASID, Blailock Design.

NURTURING HAS NO PRICE TAG

There's no getting around it: We want our kids' rooms to be fabulous because these rooms symbolize all our hopes and dreams for our children. On a rational level, we know that a perfect room won't ensure them a perfect life, but emotionally, it's a different story.

If you had your way, you'd create a castle in the air for your precious little (or not so little) one. But back here in the real world, most parents don't have unlimited time or money to devote to this important project. If you have an endless budget, the sky's the limit. But for most parents today the question is, "How can we provide rooms that nurture and protect our offspring, stimulate them, and grow along with them, without putting their college tuition in jeopardy?"

In these pages, you'll see how to create imaginative, kid-friendly looks without breaking the bank. You'll learn how an intelligently designed room can help nurture a child's development at various stages of life. You'll also see how to meet the needs (and even the wants) of several kids in the same room. Plus, we'll show you how to translate your child's personal preferences into a livable decorating scheme that won't fade from favor with the next new fad.

When planning your child's room, remember that today's open-plan homes and distinctly casual lifestyle have their roots in the human craving for closeness. So you don't need to live up to some elaborate showpiece of a bedroom. For almost the first decade of life, most children's best-loved decorating accessory is you. It's a sad child who is expected to make a fancy toy-filled room take the place of a loving adult's presence.

Any child psychologist can tell you that, from birth through the grade-school years, most children prefer to play and study in the room you're in, no matter how small or simply furnished. (Anyone who's ever tripped over toddlers in the kitchen knows how common this situation is.) So don't worry if you can't construct Sleeping Beauty's castle or a pirate ship worthy of Treasure Island in an 8×10-foot room.

Even when money is no object, elaborate theme bedrooms delight doting parents and grandparents, but they're often too static and limiting to a child's own creativity. When we remember that children do much of their developing through the

A simple mural of a castle is charming, and, when you add a blackboard to the drawbridge door, it's a creative inspiration. Buy special paint to transform any wall area into a blackboard, and frame it with a castle, jungle cave, or whatever strikes your youngster's fancy. Designer: Lynda M. Phillips, Design Sense.

exercise of their own creative and analytical processes, we can focus on providing the tools rather than the finished pieces to enhance that development.

Sure, kids clamor for everything they see on TV or at a friend's house. But many parents know the frustration of buying the latest electronic novelty toy promoted in commercials, only to have it cast aside overnight in favor of pots and pans and a pair of wooden cooking spoons or a cardboard appliance box and some crayons. The same dynamic appears when you're furnishing a whole room for a child. Focus on providing safe, sturdy furniture and play structures, easily accessible storage, and appealing colors and patterns. The kids will supply the magic of imagination.

Of course, if you're longing to hire that trompe l'oeil painter or master carpenter, go right ahead. You can still provide an inspiring framework for imaginative play. Just keep it relatively generic. A forest playhouse can house Winnie the Pooh today, Robin Hood tomorrow; a seashore mural is great for today's Little Mermaid and tomorrow's scuba diver.

COMFORT, CHALLENGE, CREATIVITY

You know you'll need a crib or bed, storage furniture, and a play/study surface, but before you invest in elaborate play equipment, consider what your child really needs.

All of childhood—some would say, all of life—is a balance between seeking safety and seeking growth. A child cannot fully grow without having easy access to a haven of comfort from which to emotionally regroup and consolidate new learning. Equally, a child can't fully enjoy the comfort provided without regular challenges that foster growth. Kids who aren't comforted enough and kids who aren't challenged enough often find life more difficult, and achieving this balance is a big day-to-day job for any parent. Fortunately, love and a sound understanding of what is appropriate to expect at

Kids love to climb, and they love little nests of their own—two reasons why bunk beds are proven favorites. This beguiling bunked castle offers plenty of comfortable sleep, storage, and play space.
Designer: Montanna & Associates.

each age go a long way. A room designed to offer plenty of comfort as well as some enjoyable challenges can help go the distance.

Everyday life takes its toll on any room where real people live, but kids are especially hard on dressed-to-impress spaces. A love of physical activity is hard-wired into kids because developing physical dexterity (both large- and small-motor skills) is essential to survival. Since the beginning of time, kids have loved to climb, peek through cutouts, and curl up inside cozy hideaways. Today, bunk beds with a safe, sturdy ladder, a hanging curtain, or a divider with peek-a-boo

A spacious, comfortable sofa and lots of space for storing toys, CDs, and more make a playroom relaxing enough for the whole family to enjoy. A blue sky ceiling and murals of cityscapes and country scenes spark young imaginations. Designer: Mojo Stumer Associates, p.c.

holes and a simple "tent" made from a small table and a sheet can easily satisfy these cravings. Kids also love to throw, lift, and build things. Lightweight toss toys work well if the room's not full of knickknacks, and all kinds of blocks and boxes let kids create structures on their own. Children with disabilities should be given play structures that let them safely enjoy these or similar skill-building activities to the fullest extent they can. Special-education professionals can offer advice on appropriate ideas and resources.

If you're fortunate enough to have a contemporary "bonus" room or an old-fashioned recreation room, make the most of it with barrier-free, all-ages equipment and furnishings. If you've got a yard, set up outdoor play structures that offer as many safe skill-building activities as your space and budget allow. Opt for a wooden play set if possible; it generally costs more than a metal set, but wooden units will age much more gracefully in your yard. Wooden units also offer the tree house option most kids adore.

If you have children of varying ages, the younger child's safety will have to be the design priority. If you can set aside a space for the older one with age-appropriate structures, that's ideal; if not, equivalent activities plus field trips can even things out. For example, a swing set with ship-style riggings to climb would be great for a seven-year-old—and potentially dangerous for a three-year-old. Tumbling mats would let both kids play full out, and trips to a local climbing wall or other big-kid activity can provide your older child with the extra challenges he or she is ready for.

Providing comfort is at least as important as providing challenges. In today's hectic world, first on the agenda should be a design that makes it easy for you to be with your child. If space allows, put an extra twin bed or a futon-style couch in your child's room. When you're up half the night with sick or fretful little ones, it's more comfortable for you and profoundly comforting for them. Or, think long-term and invest in a trundle bed, and when your child makes the move from crib to twin bed, you'll still have that extra bed when you need it. (Don't worry about an extra bed just for sleepovers, however. Most kids of all ages enjoy the novelty of camping out in a sleeping bag on a pal's floor.) A rocking chair will save your back and help you soothe an ill or frightened child. If you provide the framework for security, your child can build on it to create his or her own castles in the sky.

Preteens and teens crave the comforts of home as much as younger siblings do, but their budding independence often makes them less willing to express it. For most kids in this age range, social and academic pressures as well as other stressful situations make them seek a haven at the end of a stressful day. Preteens and teens want more privacy than younger kids do, but that doesn't mean you have to provide a phone, TV, and Internet-access computer in their bedrooms. Increasingly, experts (and many families' own experiences)

advocate keeping these portals to the outside world a bit more centrally located. Big kids do, however, need privacy to talk with friends, recharge with music and creative hobbies, and do homework without interference. They also need places to put things where they won't be disturbed by younger kids.

A room or a part of a shared room that's clearly off-limits to siblings is essential; a music system with a headset is

Beautifully crafted, well-constructed, classically designed children's furniture can be a great bargain in the long run. If you buy investment-quality pieces from the start, virtually every piece can still be on the job when your child is a teenager. Manufacturer: Brewster Wallcovering Co.

A charming mix of genuine antiques, nicely made reproductions, simple painted storage pieces, and detailed doll furnishings mingle appealingly together. The result is a room with the quiet warmth of cherished heirlooms.

dialogue will be ongoing, but if you can provide a measure of age-appropriate privacy, even teens who covet designer jeans may cheerfully bypass designer furniture. Many teens who, as youngsters, did homework at the kitchen table now are happy spreading homework out on the bed, as long as they can have their music. Good lighting for reading, a comfortable bed for nearly adult bones, and a chance to express their growing individuality make a big difference to preteens and teens.

ROOMS TO GROW ON

The last decade has seen some fantastic children's rooms, but whether you can go all out or not, think twice about spending a lot on major pieces with short-lived appeal.

If you want to create a room for your child to grow on, invest in the best-quality furniture your money allows. While home entertainment furniture may change more often to accommodate new technologies, a well-made bed, bookcase, armoire, and end table can take your child from preschool to college and beyond. (They'll also teach your child something useful about choosing quality.) If you're wondering whether better-quality furniture is worthwhile for a child's

almost as important. (Set audio level limits to prevent all-too-common hearing loss.) A family room alcove that lets young people work and play on the computer within discreet view may be a sensitive way to temper privacy with safety. The

room, divide the price of the furnishing by the estimated number of years you'll be able to use it. In many cases, the better-made classic piece will be the more economical choice in the long run. And remember, "classic" doesn't have to mean "traditional." Simple Shaker style, sturdy Mission, mid-century Modern, and romantic Victorian can all work well in a child's room. Cheerful colors, fresh fabrics, and easy-care finishes let "serious" furniture shine in your child's room. With a simple change of fabrics and colors, this same furniture will be on the job for many years to come.

Charming child-size novelty furniture abounds, and, if you've got the room, a kid-size table and chairs or a mini armchair are inviting. But a round end table and a comfy ottoman do a similar job and can be used when the child is older. Indulge the latest whims with paint, wallpaper borders, and accessories. They make a big impact and are relatively easy and inexpensive to change.

FINDING THE RIGHT FURNITURE

If you are having a difficult time finding good-quality furniture that fits your budget, check out unfinished furniture stores and ask to see their solid wood pieces. Unfinished furniture is generally lower priced than factory-finished pieces, and many of these stores sell furniture finishing products that are easier to use than ever. Some ready-to-finish furniture stores even offer how-to classes. For customers with more money than time, many of the stores will even finish chosen pieces for you.

Antique stores are also good places to find well-made beds, bureaus, and rocking chairs with a charming look, but think twice about buying an old crib or playpen; most aren't safe for babies by today's standards. Family pieces, whether they're true heirlooms or just serviceable hand-me-downs, may be good bets, though. As they did for past generations, these old pieces can carry precious memories for your children. If you're using your great-grandmother's heirloom rocking chair and it may have been painted with lead paint, be sure to have it refinished with one of today's safe lead-free finishing products.

If you end up with a mix of old, new, antique, and ready-to-finish pieces, don't fret. Some of the most charming, stylish rooms around were deliberately created this way. In fact, even affluent families that didn't inherit pieces scout flea markets and antique shops to get the look.

How to pull a disparate mix of pieces together? If your child's room is small or the pieces are frankly flea market, you can unify the look by painting most of the furniture pieces in a soothing go-with-anything hue. Fresh white, antique white, sage (gray-green), and hunter (dark green) look good with every color. (Exception: If a woodtone piece has a beautiful grain and is in good shape, just give it a clear or transparent stain finish.) Treat focal-point pieces to a custom finish to help make them stand out in the space. For example, in an Early American–style room with mostly hunter green furniture, paint the bed or armoire in barn red or antique white. A contemporary-style room with bright white furniture would look great with a bed in fire engine red or turquoise blue. (For visual balance, repeat this accent color in at least two other places, such as curtains and wall art or an area rug and rocking chair cushions.)

As long as your child is safe and comfortable, don't fret too much about getting his or her room "just right." No matter what the decorating scheme or how much you spend, you can be sure of two things: 1) Even the neatest child's toys, clothes, and paraphernalia will create a level of visual clutter that is unavoidable, and 2) The most vibrant, attractive thing in the room will always be its young occupant!

LIGHT UP THEIR LIVES

Lighting is an important element that's often neglected—and not just in kids' rooms. You'll need task lighting in several different areas, so don't try to make do with the single ceiling fixture found in many older homes. To start out, you'll be logging some hours in the rocker with bedtime stories, so be sure you have a good reading light positioned nearby. A comfortable reading spot like this will encourage your child to read for pleasure, too. A low-wattage light is helpful for midnight diaper changes, and a smaller night-light is a must-have from

Adequate general lighting is essential for safety and general navigating and playing in any child's bedroom. Just as important is task lighting for strain-free reading, studying, and working on hobbies. Just be sure to position lamps so there's no glare on a computer screen. Designer: Alla Kazovsky. Manufacturer: Kids' Studio.

a kid's point of view. A study desk needs good task lighting, but, if there's a computer in the room, position lights so there's no glare on the screen. For everyone's safety, make sure at least one light can be turned on from a wall switch by the door. Put one lamp on a dimmer switch for maximum flexibility without fuss.

SOLO ROOMS, SHARED ROOMS

Space for each child to have a room of his or her own has become the American ideal, but shared rooms are still very prevalent. Even when kids have their own rooms, they'll often play with siblings in whichever room seems handiest. A younger one may even prefer to sleep in the same room with a sibling and use his or her own room as a shared playroom. Whatever makes your children feel safe and comfortable is what's right.

Keep in mind that, while younger children have a hard time sharing things, older ones mind sharing space. If sharing a room is necessary and one or both are "big kids," be sure to create clear divisions, at least visually. If two kids of widely different ages share a room, the older one will be more bothered by the situation. To compensate, try to give the older one an extra drawer in the bathroom or an extra piece of storage furniture.

When dividing a typical bedroom, avoid decorative screens, unsecured wall units, or other pieces that may topple during the usual horseplay. Sturdy back-to-back bookcases or armoires are a smart way to create a sense of private space for each occupant, but wait until kids are old enough not to climb them. A movable curtain made of a sheet and hung on a ceiling-mounted rod can work, too. If there's only one window or the door is placed so that both sides of the room don't have easy access, you'll want to keep the room's sight lines open. In this case, you can define each

child's space with a different area rug, a higher headboard, and other subtle cues. Most useful and easy are color schemes that set off each space.

DEFINING SHARED SPACE WITH COLOR

When you ask Jamie and Jenna what colors they like and you hear "pink and purple" from one and "blue and orange" from the other, don't despair. It's true that two entirely different color schemes are usually too jarring to live with in one room and will make it look small and cluttered. But there's no reason why you can't take one color from each and add a third tone that's compatible with both for a fun look that pleases everyone. For example, pink and orange can be cooled with green for a cheery garden feeling; blue and purple can be warmed with yellow for a fresh seaside look. (We'll look more at how to tame and use lively colors in Design Primer on page 16.) Jamie's side of the room could be predominantly purple and yellow with hints of blue; Jenna's could use lots of blue and yellow with accents in purple.

Whatever the scheme, keep big furniture pieces in a soothing, space-expanding white or classic wood tones, and choose pale tints of color for the room's walls and trim. (Most paint color swatch cards show a range of lighter versions of each color. Use a tint of one favorite hue on the walls and another on the doors and trim to make everyone happy.) Lavish the favored colors full strength on everything else, from small chairs to bed ensembles. Whose is whose should be no problem!

The same color scheme can work in a children's suite, whether that's a single bedroom with adjoining bath, two rooms that share a connected bath, or, most luxurious, one or two bedrooms with a bath and adjoining playroom. As an alternative, you may want to use cool, restful colors (blue, purple, and most greens) in the bedrooms and warm, lively

White and natural woodtone furniture looks great with a few pieces in bright primary hues. Rounded corners and kid-safe paint help make this space right for little ones. When it comes to wallcoverings, the sky's the limit here. An endearing colorful alphabet border makes learning everyday fun. Manufacturer: Village, A Brand of FSC Wallcoverings.

colors (pink, orange, red, and yellow) in the playroom, with a mix of cool and warm tones in the bath set off by lots of white. Whichever approach—one scheme throughout a suite or a different scheme for each room—be sure to include a favorite color of each child.

Once you've chosen a pleasing color scheme everyone can live with, let common sense, comfort, and safety govern your purchasing decisions. When it comes to hobbies, computer games have an undeniable lure, but you can encourage more healthy mental and physical activity by providing a fuss-free space where kids can be kids. If your child loves to make music, a well-insulated space will make it easy to encourage this talent. If she paints or he makes model dinosaurs, provide wipe-clean laminate surfaces and good lighting. If horseplay is an everyday thing around your house and you have space for a real playroom, opt for recessed can lighting, thick wall-to-wall carpeting in a soil-hiding color, and comfortable chairs in a pattern that will camouflage spills and wear.

STUDY SPOTS AND BATHS

What about study areas? Given that the kitchen table may be the most appealing and a computer desk in the family room may be the safest solution for Internet searches, formal study areas in kids' rooms may not be used all the time. But for children who are easily distracted (and that's everyone when the TV is on in the same room), a quiet spot to study is a must. Good lighting that falls over the student's shoulder without a glare, a comfortable place to sit, and a work surface at the right height for writing or laptop use are just the basics. Try to indulge your child's personal preferences, however. For example, if he or she finds background music helpful, give it a try. Whatever you can do to build good study habits now will benefit your child for a lifetime.

If your home includes a bathroom to be used by children, safety will matter most. Antiscald devices on sink and tub faucets, rounded countertop corners, rugs with slip-proof backs (or no rugs if your floors are heated), a rubber-footed stool for the littlest ones, and grab bars as towel bars are sensible options. (Grab bars need to be reinforced with wood blocks anchored to wall studs, so if you're rehabbing the bathroom or building a new one, plan grab bars in from the start.) Beyond that, indulge in whatever decorative flights of fancy your child enjoys. If the bathroom is part of a bedroom suite, you may want to continue the bedroom's color scheme or reverse it: For example, a mostly blue bedroom with some yellow accents and a predominantly yellow bath with blue accents.

A lot is demanded of your child's room—and of any room in which children will spend much time. It has been many years since children were seen and not heard or were judged as small adults with big shortcomings, but a kid-friendly home doesn't have to mean wall-to-wall crayons and chaos. Chil-

A stool for reaching the sink is a must-have in a bathroom for your little one. The pretty yellow complements the cool blue walls of the bedroom; tile in vibrant hues ties the suite together. Designer: Lynn Pries, Lynn Pries Designs.

dren from cradle to college need structure, consistency, and routines as much as adults do, and a well-planned room can help. Creating a home environment that welcomes and accepts children without sacrificing the needs of adults can be a challenge. But what family project is more rewarding, year after year?

Design Primer

Whats more important than a memorable room? For a child, it's a comfortable, workable space that grows smoothly along with him or her. Keeping the "fun" in "functional" can be a challenge, as every age group has its own needs. Luckily, most kids go through fairly predictable stages, and you can provide for these developments and create personally expressive, attractive spaces at the same time. Best of all, you don't need to invest in all new elements to give your child's room a fresh look that will provide delight and comfort for years to come.

Two snug curtained berths like those found in train sleeper compartments bring back a sense of adventure every kid craves. The coral, cream, and lime color scheme is full of personality, too. Drawers, hooks, and shelves offer lots of storage that's easy to use.

Ample windows transform an ordinary-size shared space into a bright, open environment that gives both kids some psychological breathing room. A dreamy ceiling mural keeps the open-air feeling going, even at nighttime.

BEDROOM BASICS

Space may be the last real luxury, but, in many parts of the world, even parents don't have the luxury of a private bedroom. In most individual-oriented Western cultures, however, private spaces are considered important even for youngsters. In the United States, open-plan homes that blend family rooms with kitchens exist side by side with master bedroom suites and dedicated children's wings. The pull between togetherness and privacy is constant—and perfectly natural. While a bedroom of one's own may be the American ideal, many children find a shared room less lonely, and they contentedly share bedrooms as long as their own turf within the room is clearly marked. Ingenious furniture designs, such as the clever loft bed with drawers and desk space below or the trundle bed with a pull-out bed for guests, can make just about any size space workable.

If generous square footage isn't essential in a child's room, what is? Natural light from at least one fair-size window, for one thing. Sunlight aids the absorption of vitamin D and can alleviate the winter-borne depression called Seasonal Affective Disorder (SAD). It also makes any room look and feel larger and airier. You can multiply the effect of windows with strategically placed mirrors, but make sure they are unbreakable or wait until children are old enough not to whack mirrors during play. For shared rooms, try to provide equal access to the window (but be certain to outfit it with safety bars to make sure no one can fall or climb out; screens don't count). Avoid heavy, elaborate window treatments that attract dust and can tempt youngsters into potentially dangerous hanging stunts. Instead, you may want to choose simple, washable curtains or shades (be sure to keep cords on halyards or cleats high out of reach). Room-darkening shades, the kind found in hotel rooms, may be helpful for reluctant nappers.

Obviously, another essential is the door and safe access to it. Kids need to be able to easily find and reach the bedroom door, even half-asleep, in case of an emergency or just for midnight trips to the bathroom. Make sure furniture does not obstruct the doorway, and be militant about having kids keep a clutter-free path from the bed to the door. (Even if they're nimble enough to keep from falling, you may not be!) A night-light is important for safety as well as for psychological comfort, and many are available with tiny shades depicting everything from a protective angel to the latest cartoon character.

If your child's room is located near stairs, especially a dramatic open staircase, be sure that railings are high enough to protect the big kids from falling over and that vertical rails are close enough to prevent small ones from slipping through.

KID-FRIENDLY FABRICS

From a traditional look with lace curtains and coordinating drapes and bedding to the color extravaganza featured in contemporary Skä style, nothing pulls a look together like fabric. Colors, patterns, and textures are virtually limitless, and because fabric can be used in a variety of ways, it's one of the easiest design elements for do-it-yourselfers to incorporate into a decor. Yet many parents cringe at the thought of using fabric throughout their child's room—especially if it's expensive. The bad news? Whatever you cover, drape, or wrap with fabric is bound to get worn or stained. The good news, however, is that many of today's fabrics are pretreated or can be treated with a stain-resistant coating. For high-traffic spots like bedding and side chairs, choose fabrics that can be washed or easily cleaned. The following checklist is a helpful guide for choosing kid-friendly fabrics.

Fabric	Durability	Weight	Care	Best Use
Corduroy	Adds fabulous texture to a room without sacrificing durability. Holds up to repeated use; after several washings, however, it can appear comfortably worn.	Medium and heavy	Wash for a soft finish; dry-clean to prevent crushed pile.	Cushions, headboards, ottomans, upholstery for chairs and couches
Cotton	Versatile and decorative, cotton comes in an unlimited selection of colors and patterns.	Light	Wash fabric before sewing to prevent future shrinkage.	Curtains and drapes, cushions, dust ruffles, duvets and bedspreads, headboards, pillows and shams, Roman blinds, slipcovers, upholstery for chairs and couches
Cotton Chintz/ Polished	Popular and affordable, its shiny finish actually repels dust, but this same sheen can also fade after several cleanings.	Light	Wash before sewing to prevent future shrinkage. Dry-clean to retain shiny finish.	Curtains and drapes, cushions, dust ruffles, duvets and bedspreads, headboards, pillows and shams, Roman blinds, slipcovers
Denim	Tough and practically maintenance free, denim has long-lasting durability.	Medium and heavy	Treat stains as you would for denim clothing, and machine wash.	Cushions, dust ruffles, duvets and coverlets, headboards, ottomans, pillows and shams, upholstery for chairs and couches
Lace	Fine laces should be used sparingly as they are susceptible to wear and tear. Laces with polyester content are more durable.	Light	Machine wash on gentle cycle or hand wash; hang to dry.	Curtains, cushions, dust ruffles, pillows
Velvet	Lends a plush, luxurious feel to any decor, and, with its tight weave, it can be quite durable. Choose a quality fabric for high-traffic upholstery and soft furnishings.	Heavy	Better velvets must be dry-cleaned. Iron on low heat to prevent scorching fabric.	Drapes, headboards, ottomans, pillows and shams, tablecloths
Vinyl	Because of its long-lasting durability, vinyl is one of the easiest—and most affordable—fabrics to use in a child's room.	Heavy	Clean by wiping with damp cloth; cannot be machine washed. NEVER IRON.	Headboards, large floor cushions, ottomans, stool and bench covers, tablecloths

You can disguise the odd angles and eaves of an attic room or play off of them to create a lighthearted child's space. This cheerful circus-inspired nook offers plenty of room to play as well as to study and sleep. A big dormer window is key to dispelling gloom.

Safety isn't at the top of the mind with most children, so it needs to be with you.

Closet doors that swing open waste space in a small bedroom. Sliding closet doors on tracks don't take up as much floor space, but they can be heavy and hard for youngsters to move. In either case, you may want to replace these types of doors with pocket doors if the budget allows. Or, simpler yet, use a pair of drapery-length curtains on a tension rod instead of traditional closet doors. You can make washable cotton-polyester blend curtains easily and affordably from twin-size sheets, with the added bonus of coordinating the curtains with your child's bed linens. A closet that kids can easily use is one that they are more likely to use—instead of the floor.

Clutter may be a matter of opinion, but general cleanliness is important to children's health because their immune systems are not as robust or well-developed as most adults'. Plan on easy-to-clean hard surfaces and fully washable—not just spot-cleanable—soft surfaces throughout the room.

If your child has allergies, his or her pediatrician or an allergist can advise you on specific ways to reduce allergens in your child's room and elsewhere in your home. In general, avoid lots of knickknacks, aptly dubbed "dust catchers," unless the items are truly dear to your child. As children grow up, they often accumulate more and more items they find

FURNITURE TRANSFORMATIONS

A threadbare ottoman gathering dust in your attic. A beat-up trunk full of old clothes in the corner of your garage. A little-used china cabinet in your dining room. Indeed, some of the best furniture and accessory finds for children's rooms are already right in your own home! By thinking creatively, many traditional furnishings you have on hand or those found in a garage sale or secondhand store can be transformed into spectacular pieces for kids. Read this clever list of possibilities for inspiration, and you'll soon be embarking on an all-out treasure hunt!

Mirror, Mirror

Old window sashes and iron grates can become interesting mirrors for children's rooms. To refurbish, keep any glass intact. Clean frames, and paint as desired (don't worry about painting over glass). When dry, take frame to a glass shop to have glass panes removed and mirrors installed. Also ask to have a hanger attached to the back, especially if the frame is metal. If the frame is wood, you can install your own hanger by attaching eye screws securely and evenly on each side on the back of the frame. Thread picture wire through the screws, and secure to form a hanger.

Light up Your Life

An inexpensive lamp converter kit from a home supply store can turn anything from wood newel posts to plastic piggy banks into unique bedside lamps. For the lamp base, choose items 12 inches high or taller to ensure proper lighting. (Items with a hollow center are easy to work with.) Follow manufacturer's instructions to install the lamp. Then top the lamp with a store-bought shade, or customize your own by purchasing a plain shade and decorating it with coordinating trims (buttons, pom-poms, rickrack, fringe, etc.).

Treasure Trove

Turn an army trunk or a steamer trunk into an oversize toy box. For an adventurous look, leave the trunk's shabby chic appearance intact, especially if the paint or paper has worn to a muted patina or if old travel stickers and name tags are visible. If the outside is papered, remove any loose paper, and apply a heavy coat of white glue to prevent future peeling. For wood exteriors, simply sand smooth, paint the chest as desired, then add your own designs to the outside.

For safety, be sure to reinforce or replace hinges and remove the hinge on the front lock that fastens the trunk shut. Clean out the inside of the trunk, removing any fabric lining, and paint it a dark color to disguise crayon marks and scuffs. To keep little fingers from being smashed by the lid, you might want to make a wood wedge for each side. Cut 2 small pieces of wood trim, each about 1 inch long and the same width as the top edge of the trunk. Glue 1 side of a Velcro hook and loop fastener to the bottom of each wood piece and the other side of the fastener to the top edge of the trunk on both sides, about 3 inches from the trunk's back edge.

Cheery Chairs

Wood chairs have a variety of uses in a child's room. Tiny chairs can be hung on walls and used as display shelves. Or, stash a slatback dining room chair in a walk-in closet or a bathroom for a childsize valet. A large chair with a decorative back can sit beside a bed, doing double duty as a bookshelf or catchall. The best chairs for such uses are sturdy, with pop-out seats. If the chair creaks or wiggles at the joints, reinforce with wood glue. Strip and sand old paint, then coat with at least 2 layers of paint. Finish as desired. To recover pop-out seats, remove old fabric, then replace batting and staple it to the underside of the chair seat to secure. Cover with vinyl, canvas, or another fabric by wrapping sides and corners to underside of chair seat; staple in place.

Outrageous Ottomans

An oversize ottoman is just the right size for a child. If you're lucky enough to have 2 matching ottomans, use them side by side at the foot of a bed or on either side as bedside tables. Ottomans can also be used as valets or stools for small vanities and tables. Most ottomans are upholstered, and, if yours has extensive tufting and trim, you may want to hire a professional to reupholster it. If the decoration is minimal, you can reupholster it yourself by carefully removing old fabric and using the pieces as a pattern for new fabric. Sew as needed to create the cover, then tack, sew, or glue your new fabric in place. Finish with contrasting, fun trims. If your ottoman has wooden legs, refinish and paint them first before reupholstering.

Creative Cupboards

Dark, oversize armoires and china cabinets can be transformed into functional storage space for a child's room. The first thing to do is completely strip or sand the piece of furniture, remove all hardware, and repair any loose hinges or other damaged areas. Reinforce inside shelving, and reglue the drawer joints if needed to strengthen. Paint the inside and outside of the cabinet in bright, cheerful colors. Or, use a contrasting color scheme to match the room's decor, and add interesting elements such as wallpaper cutouts, painted checkerboard borders, full-length stripes, and other decorative finishes to make the piece lively and fun.

If you don't want a glass-door cabinet in a young child's room, replace the glass with gathered fabric or chicken wire for a charming country look. Designer: Maria Myers. Manufacturer: Chic Shack.

If the piece has glass doors, you can remove the glass and stretch chicken wire across the opening on the inside, nailing small wood trim over the wire's sharp ends. Another option is to mount gathered curtains made from fabric used elsewhere in the room on tension rods on the inside of the doors. Remove shelves as needed to create functional storage space for computer monitors, baskets of toys, or books.

Hob Knobs

Antique doorknobs can be turned into darling bed finials, tie backs for drapery, or even hooks for hanging towels. Even better, the knobs don't have to match. Clean all knobs before use. If they are rusty or chipped, you can paint them with oilbase paint. Let dry, then adhere small paper cutouts to centers of knobs with clear-drying craft glue. Finish with a clear protective varnish.

For hooks, evenly space knobs along the center of a painted piece of pine shelving cut to desired length and width. Fasten the board to a bathroom or bedroom wall. Use the same technique for creating drapery tiebacks, but use a small square piece of wood and only 1 knob for each tieback. For bed finials, simply attach a knob to the top of each finial, drilling a hole if needed and securing with wood glue.

Wipe-clean laminates make for easy-care craft project and play surfaces, but they're also wonderfully expressive of your own creative decorating impulses. Available in hundreds of colors and patterns, they make any playroom colorful and carefree.

meaningful, so make friends with a little empty space, simplify cleanup, and be sure to leave plenty of room for tomorrow's treasures.

Stealing Space: Upstairs, Downstairs

While you'll want a conventional room for a young child's sleeping room, you can get more creative when it comes to carving out a play space. A basement, an attic, or even a spacious stair landing (with appropriate gates in front of the stairs) can yield space for a kid-friendly playroom. Teens looking for a private space away from younger siblings may want to claim a part of the basement or the attic as their bedroom, and, as long as they can get out quickly in an emergency, this solution can ease a space crunch.

In general, attics tend to be the hottest parts of the house, so you may want to paint walls in cool, pale blues and greens. If the room has awkward alcoves and low walls in some areas, you can employ a designer's trick and camouflage them with a small all-over print wallcovering. Coordinating bookcases in several sizes can give an integrated look to storage on walls of different heights. To keep bookcases from visually overwhelming the space, consider painting them a pale tint to match the walls. The attic is a perfect place for small-scale furniture, from bona fide children's tables and chairs to easygoing beanbag seating. If your kids are younger, gate the stairwell, and, whatever their ages, make sure you have plenty of strategically placed light fixtures, especially near the stairs.

Unless they have a walkout feature like a sliding glass door, basements tend to be dark and gloomy. To lighten them up, consider painting basement walls a light, warm color like creamy white, soft yellow, or peach. If your basement has old wood paneling from the rec room era, you can paint it if it's real wood. For a visually light effect that retains the interesting wood grain, consider pickling or whitewashing the wood. If your basement walls are plastic faux wood, it will be hard to paint them successfully, so you'll be better off taking down the paneling and painting the walls. (If the walls underneath the panels are in poor shape, fix any major problems and camouflage the minor ones with stylish stucco-type textured paint.) If you've got even one unflawed, smooth wall, consider painting it with special blackboard paint, and buy a box of colored chalk. Even big kids will enjoy it!

Basements and attics are great for messy, noisy hobbies you don't want to have take over the family room or other parts of your domain. Laminate surfaces and vinyl tile floors make paint-and-glue projects easy to clean up, and sound-insulating ceiling panels keep your garage band indoors and your neighborly relations intact. Kids can camp out, playact, and generally be kids!

Chic Child-Wise Choices

You want your child's new room to look fresh and current, even if the furniture you're using isn't all brand-new. Luckily, what really distinguishes an okay room from a wonderful room is consistency, functionality, and personality. These qualities don't require a huge budget, but they do call for some planning.

Consistency just means you come up with a color scheme and a visual theme and maintain them throughout the room. For example, if you start out with blue, peach, plaids, and seashells, don't throw in (or neglect to remove) items that feature pink, black, florals, and zebras. The smaller the room, the more important consistency will be in preventing a cluttered look. You're not trying to be rigid here; you're trying to create a bit of underlying visual order that will stand up to the multitude of everyday kid items that will soon be scattered around.

Unless you're starting from scratch, the first and often toughest part of a decorating job may be editing—that is, removing pieces from the room that don't support the new vision. Of course, there are a couple of important exceptions.

If an accessory is meaningful to your child, do your best to find a place for it in the new room scheme. Sometimes just grouping a treasured white elephant with other accessories will keep it visible but not annoyingly prominent. Kids' toys are so varied in style and color, just about anything can work in the mix.

Functionality is a simple concept: Does every piece in the room serve an essential need? A comfortable place to sleep, a convenient place to play, an accessible place to store toys and clothing, and a workable place to study or indulge in hobbies are the basics. Once you've found them, it's time to inject the magic ingredient of personality.

Choose two or three compatible colors your child likes and stick with them to create a look that's easy to live with. An analogous color scheme of red, purple, and blue makes a strong yet harmonious statement in this mostly white room. Designer: Maria Myers. Manufacturer: Chic Shack.

Suppose you've inherited a piece of furniture that is safely designed, well-made, and basic to a bedroom, but, cosmetically, it doesn't appeal to you or your youngster. Obviously, you could start shopping around for something new, but you could also consider refinishing the piece to work better with your new room scheme. Custom finishing can not only enhance the visual consistency you're seeking, but it is also one of the best ways to add the pizzazz of personality to a particular furniture piece.

You can unite a whole houseful of unmatched hand-me-downs in a charming way by painting or finishing them the same. (If you want a few pieces to be different, keep in mind

FRESHENING FURNITURE

Refinishing furniture is one of the most exciting aspects of decorating. A tired, worn chest can be spruced up to look completely new; a unique finish can totally transform a blasé armoire into a stunning period piece. The best part is that refinishing furniture can save you lots of money—especially if you purchase pieces from a secondhand store or refinish pieces you already have on hand. Refinishing furniture can require a lot of time—if you want to do it correctly—but the process itself is quite simple.

Safety First

Like other rooms in your home, a child's room has special concerns, specifically those related to safety and durability. Most paint and special finishes you choose for furniture are suitable for children, provided they are sealed with a protective coating to prevent chipping and peeling. Additionally, today's paints do not have the harmful chemicals found in their older counterparts. Still, if you like the weathered look of an antique piece of furniture, it is important to make sure that its painted finish does not contain lead. Lead, both its dust and chips, can contaminate your home and cause serious health problems for you and your family. Obviously, any furniture with lead paint should be stripped or discarded. To confirm lead content, purchase an easy-to-use swab from a home supply store. When applied to a painted surface containing lead, the end will turn pink. If you decide to strip the piece, wear a respirator and work outdoors.

Please note: Whether you are refinishing wood, metal, or plastic, begin with a clean surface so the finish will adhere properly and evenly. Make any necessary repairs, and remove all hardware. Wear rubber gloves, protective goggles, and work outdoors if possible.

REFINISHING WOOD SURFACES

What You'll Need

MINERAL SPIRITS, WAX REMOVER, OR COMMERCIAL WOOD CLEANER
GEL OR LIQUID PAINT STRIPPER
PAINTBRUSHES
FLAT SCRAPER
STEEL WOOL
WOOD FILLER
SANDPAPER
CLEAN, DAMP CLOTH
STAIN-BLOCKING PRIMER
WATERBASE PAINT OR SPRAY PAINT

1. For painted wood, use mineral spirits, wax remover, or commercial wood cleaner to thoroughly clean surface. Let dry.

2. Apply liquid or gel stripper according to manufacturer's instructions. When old finish begins to bubble, scrape off old paint, following wood grain and taking care not to gouge or scratch surface. Repeat until all paint has been removed. Use steel wool on any stubborn areas.

3. Fill any holes or blemishes with wood filler, let dry, then lightly sand following wood grain. Wipe away dust with a clean, slightly damp cloth.

4. If you plan to paint the piece, prime it according to manufacturer's instructions. Use wide paintbrush, and make long, even strokes. Let dry completely.

5. Apply 2 coats of paint to furniture, letting it dry between coats. If knots or blemishes still show through, apply a third coat.

REFINISHING METAL SURFACES

What You'll Need

WIRE BRUSH OR STEEL WOOL
IRON OXIDE PRIMER
PAINTBRUSHES
SPRAY PAINT OR WIDE PAINTBRUSH AND PAINT FOR METAL

1. Most of the old layers of paint and rust on metal furniture can be removed by scrubbing with a firm wire brush or steel wool. Rub until surface is smooth, then wash with water. Let dry.

2. Apply iron oxide primer, which inhibits rust, to surface. Let dry.

3. For quick finishes and for furniture with filigree or other small decorative features, spray paint provides complete coverage and is easy to apply. Hold can about 12 inches away from surface, lightly spray, and let dry. Repeat until all metal is covered. For large metal surfaces or if you have a custom paint color in mind, use a brush to apply paint in thin coats. Let dry between each coat.

REFINISHING PLASTIC SURFACES

What You'll Need

SPONGE OR PLASTIC SCRUB PAD
LIQUID HOUSEHOLD DETERGENT
BLEACH (OPTIONAL)
SPRAY PAINT

1. Using a sponge or plastic scrub pad, clean plastic furniture with a mixture of warm water and detergent. To remove mildew, add a capful of bleach to water mixture.

2. Spray paint adheres well to plastic and is the easiest type of paint to apply. Hold can about 12 inches away from surface, lightly spray, and let dry. Repeat until entire surface has even coverage.

Well-made heirlooms can be as sturdy as any furniture you'd buy today—or even more so. If time has taken its toll on your old treasures, a furniture restorer can bring them back to life for another generation to enjoy. Just consult an expert before replacing parts on significant antiques.

that, in general, a smaller, more delicately scaled piece, such as a rocking chair, looks less oppressive in a dark wood finish than a chest of drawers or another massive piece does. A big piece takes up less space visually if it's finished in a light, cool color.)

If you are missing some key pieces or would like to start fresh with pieces you can customize, consider ready-to-finish (often called "unfinished") furniture. Many ready-to-finish furniture specialty stores offer solid hardwood furniture you can finish (or have the store finish) for a custom look. Most also offer specialty pieces for children.

If you have your heart set on heirlooms but didn't inherit any, antique shops can yield wonderful beds as well as dressers, armoires, rocking chairs, and toy chests. Porcelain doll dishes, wood rocking horses, and other quality toys are also available. Resale shops and flea markets also can be worthwhile sources, but you'll have to sift through finds more carefully to discover the good stuff.

If you're starting out with family hand-me-downs, resale shop finds, or unfinished pieces, edit until you're left with only those that offer good function and durable construction. If your budget is more flexible, head for one of the better conventional (factory-finished) furniture stores. These stores offer a full range of juvenile furniture pieces that conform to the latest safety regulations as well as offer furnishings your child won't outgrow.

Whether you are shopping in a furniture store or in Grandma's attic, be sure to check for quality construction. If you want to invest in pieces your child can enjoy now and hand down as family heirlooms later, hardwood pieces with doweled (not just stapled and glued) construction are a solid bet. Look inside drawers to see if the fronts are held on with dovetails. Lean or pull gently on a piece to see if it's sturdy and stable not shaky. (If you're shopping online you can't do this last test, but you can check for furniture descriptions that mention "doweled" or "dovetail" construction. Don't settle for less.)

Heirloom-quality furniture may be crafted of solid hardwood or made of hardwood that is veneered with another, usually costlier, hardwood. Don't be afraid of veneers in general; just be sure they are securely applied to hardwood underneath. Used since early times, veneering makes using luxurious woods more affordable. Both solid wood and wood veneers on hardwood offer the kind of quality that lasts.

Your retailer can explain quality construction methods that also further the useful life of furniture. Be sure to ask about extra safety measures in the case of bunk beds (ladders,

Whether in brass or painted wrought iron, traditionally styled metal beds add a nostalgic, romantic feeling. An openwork design keeps the bed's visual impact light, so it doesn't overwhelm a small bedroom. You can repaint iron beds for a totally different look: A tailored style like this would be dramatic painted red or black.

safety rails, etc.), cribs (distance between bars), and toy chests (safety hinges).

Wherever you shop, be very careful to check each piece thoroughly to make sure it's safe for your child. In general, plan to retrofit any vintage cribs with additional bars; check metal pieces for sharp edges; stay away from old stuffed animals, mattresses, and other fabric items that cannot be thoroughly washed; and steer clear of items with small detachable pieces that pose a choking hazard for kids under age five.

To protect against the hazards of old flaking lead paint (illegal since 1978), be sure to wear a safety mask and gloves, and follow safety recommendations for removing paint. (Basically, remove it with appropriate solvent; don't try to sand it off, and don't even be around the project if you're pregnant.) If it's a valuable antique and you like the look of the original finish, find out whether you can have a clear urethane sealant applied without lowering the value. If not, keep the real antiques for adult rooms, and explore quality reproductions for kids.

Look Beyond the Woods

Another way to inject personality into a room full of wood furniture is with a metal bed. Available in brass, iron, powder-coated steel, and other metals in a range of styles from elaborately traditional to sleekly modern, metal beds make great focal points. As with any product made for children, sturdy construction is very important, so shop around, ask questions, and review manufacturer's information before you buy. Look for pieces with rounded corners and completely smooth finishes; the "burrs" (rough edges on metal pieces) can be sharp.

To balance the room, add another piece or two of metal furniture—perhaps a night table or an occasional chair. In a traditional room, a little round ice cream parlor table and coordinating round-seated sweetheart chairs offer nostalgic charm, and their small scale lets them fit just about anywhere. If you don't find the metal accent pieces you like in conventional furniture stores, look in outdoor and casual furniture stores for appealing designs in powder-coated aluminum or iron.

Beds and coordinating storage furniture are also available in other materials, from romantic wicker (including easy-care "all weather" wicker) to rustic peeled logs for a pioneer cabin look. Because these materials are inherently interesting, they'll appeal to kids now and go the distance a lot better than many juvenile designs. Today's fairy princess abode in wicker can become tomorrow's tropical getaway for a teen; a peeled log pioneer fort can become a fishing lodge-inspired hangout tomorrow.

Pink, orange, yellow, and purple make a hot combo that appeals to girls of all ages. For a boy, bright red could replace the pink, and the good vibrations would stay the same. Cool the look with lots of clean white, light gray, or another neutral. Manufacturer: PJ Kids.

PINK AND BLUE AND MORE

Not too long ago, a little girl's room was predictably pink and preferably ruffled; her brother's was blue or some combination of suitably masculine colors, such as blue and red. For patterns, girls had florals, boys had geometrics, and never the twain could meet.

Today, it's another story. Girls are as likely as boys to enjoy blue plaids, and, while American boys are still more socially constrained in their choices, a jungle-theme room for boys could include exotic blooms as well as carnivores. Led by innovative European designers and inspired both by nature and the many cultures around the world, children's products,

from toys to school supplies to furnishings, are available in a great range of brilliant colors. You can expect to find exotic orange, purple, yellow, and green as prominent as traditional red and blue. In such a fun-loving rainbow of hues, even the occasional tropical pink or light purple can make a unisex appearance—very useful when you're creating shared playrooms and bathrooms.

Of course, many boys and girls do prefer traditional color schemes and visual themes, and it's easier than ever to indulge them with today's great products. The important thing is that your child's room reflect his or her own personal preferences—not some stereotypical "correct" look. You may have a budding Michelangelo or Marie Curie on your hands, and you'll want his or her room to nurture that authentic spirit as much as possible. There will be time enough to deal with the standardization that comes from peer pressure in the preteen and teen years.

If you're not sure where your young child's interests will lie or you want to ensure that a decorating scheme will appeal to girls and boys of all ages, you can't go wrong with a nature-inspired scheme. From preschoolers to preteens and even beyond, kids feel an affinity with the natural world and enjoy anything related to it. Dogs, horses, and jungle creatures are especially popular with both sexes. Farms and forests also yield flexible motifs that can grow along with your child.

SPECIAL ISSUES FOR EVERY AGE-GROUP

You may not be able to check off everything on your child's (or your own!) wish list, but there are a few key needs for each age-group that you should focus on.

ROCK-A-BYE BABIES

Babies' needs are crucial but simple—a safe nest to sleep in, a safe place to have diapers changed, and a comfortable spot

A changing table with open lower shelves keeps diapers, supplies, and clothing at the ready without fumbling—important when you've got a wiggly little one on your hands. Lower shelves can stash toys where toddlers can easily reach them without climbing. Stylist: Amy Leonard. Manufacturer: The Glidden Company.

for you to sit while feeding, cuddling, and rocking him or her. In fact, a comfy rocking or gliding chair is as important as a bed and changing table. Scientific research has shown that babies actually need a lot of cuddling in order to thrive, physically as well as mentally. If you are a new parent, you'll probably be tired and stressed, so make it as easy as possible to spend cheek-to-cheek time with your baby. You'll both be healthier!

Babies sleep most of the time, so a comfortable bed is a must. A bassinet or cradle may be charming, but it's only safe for a few months before babies start moving and rolling. If you do use a bassinet, be sure it's on a sturdy base that won't move. If you're using a cradle, make sure the cradle won't rock more than a few inches either way so that baby and all don't fall. A more practical solution may be a well-made crib; you can swaddle a young infant to give him or her the comforting sense of being in a smaller enclosure. (Don't fill the bed with stuffed animals and pillows, though. Except at playtime, confine the soft stuff to securely tied bumper pads and relatively thin blankets that won't pose a smothering hazard. Babies can often get themselves into situations they can't get out of!)

A changing table will get a lot of use, so be sure to get a good one. You can make a changing table out of a waist-high chest of drawers, but be sure you add a top with a low guardrail as well as a waterproof pad. A chest may be more versatile later, but it generally is not as safe and, therefore, not recommended. In addition, diapers and clothes will be easier to reach if you opt for a changing table with open shelves below. Choose a unit with a safety strap to go across baby's middle, or make sure you can get at things you need with one hand while keeping the other on your little wiggly worm at all times.

To aid with midnight feedings and diaper changing, use an overhead light on a dimmer that you can switch on from the door for your safety's sake. Choose a room-darkening shade to facilitate daytime naps.

When it's time to decorate walls, remember that, until they're between six and nine months old, babies can't see subtle colors and details. Black-and-white and other strongly contrasting colors work better as do simple patterns. A proven favorite is two dots and a curve within a circle that suggests human eyes and smiling mouth.

If you don't care for vivid color schemes, choose a pastel you'd like to use longer term and pair it with a dark or bright accent hue you can change when your child gets a bit older. Another option is simply to stick with more restful pastel hues throughout the room and provide visual stimulation with age-appropriate toys.

Although newborn babies' sight may be lacking, their hearing and sense of touch are almost fully developed at birth. Indulge them with safe toys in a variety of textures and soft melodic sounds. Crib toys and mobiles that move or play music will appeal to most babies as well as add attractive color and pattern to the room. Just make sure that any hanging toys your baby can reach are safe and that they do not have small detachable parts.

Toddlers: Out on the Town

Babies who are old enough to crawl, let alone toddle, are at their most challenging in terms of safety. At this stage they can perceive colors better than infants, but they still lack the ability to understand, say, a storybook scene on a wall. Keep things simple for awhile yet, and concentrate on making sure every square inch is clean and safe. For example, no hanging tablecloths, no exposed electrical outlets, no breakable or heavy items on tables and shelves, and no sharp corners on any furniture.

Tots making the transition from crawling to toddling will use any available vertical item to pull themselves up, so choose furniture pieces that are sturdy and stable. For the inevitable tumbles, make sure floors are clean and resilient or softly covered with carpeting or rugs. If you don't have wall-to-wall carpeting, use slip-proof pads under every rug. Vinyl resilient tiles and wood flooring are more forgiving than ceramic tile or stone, but nonslip rugs can make a real difference on any floor.

Depending on how active or how tall your child is, you may want to make the transition to a low youth bed now. If there's even a chance your child can climb out of the crib, it's time to move on.

Perceptive Preschoolers

Somewhere around age two, children start perceiving colors and details more and their ability to move around and explore is up and running full tilt. At this point, you can indulge yourself and your little one in decorations that feature storybook or cartoon characters, but don't invest a lot unless your budget is ample, as tastes change often at this age. Keep safety in mind, and avoid decorative items with small parts—anything reachable will be subjected to a taste test!

Toddlers exploring on unsteady legs need lots of soft landing spots, so a thick carpet or plush area rug with a nonslip pad can really help. Choose sturdy furniture with rounded edges for happy adventuring.

If your child hasn't left the crib yet, now's probably the time. Youth beds are available in a variety of amusing forms, from sports cars to rocket ships, but their appeal may be limited and their quality is often questionable. If you don't like faddish toddler beds but are worried about putting your child into a full-height twin bed, a practical alternative is to simply put a good-quality twin box spring and mattress on the floor. For the year or two you'll be using it, this interim solution may be easiest. A colorful, washable comforter and bed linens make the look complete.

A loft bed doesn't have to have a second berth below. Some of the cleverest use the lower space for a desk and shipshape storage drawers, bins, and shelves. A youngster can stash a lot of stuff in a configuration like this and still have floor space aplenty for active play. Retailer: Gautier USA, Inc.

Toy storage is paramount at this age. Kids accumulate lots of playthings but are easily overwhelmed by even simple cleanup efforts. Make things easier on yourself and on them with lots of low, open storage bins, baskets, and shelves. Choose pieces with smooth surfaces and rounded corners for safety's sake. Under-the-bed storage drawers on wheels are another practical option to help keep less-used items available but not underfoot. A classic toy chest with a flat top can provide ample storage plus an extra play surface. (Just make sure to reinforce hinges and remove lock.) A low chest of drawers is usually sufficient for storing young children's clothes, but you may also want to provide a few low, rounded pegs to make quick work of hanging jackets, overalls, and robes. Hangers are a hassle for youngsters, so plan to hang dressy outfits yourself or provide extra pegs so kids can help.

At this age, children want to play wherever you are, so have some good-looking, easily accessible baskets for collecting toys that tend to end up all over the house. If you have the space, dedicate some low shelves for toys in the family room. If space is too limited, a couple of large handsome baskets stationed in the family room can make short work of cleanup.

In the family room or in their own rooms, children this age will happily play on the floor, so make sure it's still as clean and comfortable as when they were crawling and falling. Wall-to-wall carpeting offers great comfort but can take a beating with craft projects. Consider layering a washable rug or two, or use nonslip rugs on top of easy-to-clean resilient or wood flooring. (Don't use carpeting remnants over carpets or rugs; the rough burlap backing will damage the underlying carpet.) Avoid very dark or very light solid color rugs and carpets that show every spill and stain; opt for midtone hues with some gray, brown, or taupe undertones. For example, choose olive green instead of lime green, royal blue instead of baby blue, teal instead of turquoise blue, burgundy instead of bright red, and mauve or antique rose instead of pink. A strongly patterned rug in midrange jewel tones, including just about any Oriental rug, will hide stains even better and add timeless style.

A child-size table and chairs come into their own for this age-group. Charming affordable sets abound at ready-to-finish furniture shops, and pieces you customize now may be treasured for generations. A small table can become a lamp table later; small chairs work as timeless accessories to hold potted plants on the porch or a colorful stack of towels in the bath. If space or budgets are tight, a round-cornered end table and a footstool or ottoman can stand in as pint-size furniture, as long as the seat and table height are right. Let your child try it out: Make sure there's enough table surface to spread out projects and that the child's feet fully touch the floor.

To complete the room, station a small additional table at bedside to hold a lamp and storybook. A floor lamp is an alternative if space is tight, but be sure it has a heavyweight base to keep it from tipping over during boisterous play, and don't use halogen lights where children can reach them (they are dangerously hot).

Children ages two to five are mentally developed enough to have scary thoughts and feelings, but most still don't have the ability to distinguish real from fantasy information. Even if you are vigilant about protecting them from violent or menacing images on television shows and movies, little ones often find nighttime very frightening. To ensure adequate sleep, close closet doors, put on a small night-light, and pro-

vide a security blanket or another "lovie" to cuddle with. These usually count more than all the adorable accessories in the world.

ON-THE-GROW GRADE-SCHOOLERS

In the early grade-school years, roughly ages six to eight, children have more opinions about room decor and can begin to articulate what they like in a way that you can use. The line between reality and fantasy is still blurred at this age, so you'll need to interpret and help them compromise. If your child wants a tree house to sleep in, a bunk bed customized with a trompe l'oeil rendering of leafy trees gives this childhood dream practical expression. The latest movie or cartoon hero plays big at this age, and all you may need is an easily strippable wallpaper border and a coordinating toss pillow to make the grade.

By age six, most kids are able to safely use bunk beds and loft beds, but be sure upper berths have safety rails on both sides and that the mattress sits well below the top of the rail. If space is tight, loft beds with storage and a desk configuration below make a clever solution kids will love. Because they're double-decker, you can usually fit two such structures into even a small shared bedroom.

Sleepovers start becoming important for young grade-schoolers, so consider how you'll accommodate these visitors. A trundle bed is ideal, but an inflatable air mattress or even a sleeping bag on an area rug will often do the trick. (Be sure to have a night-light in the bedroom and bath plus a lighted path to the bathroom for the comfort and safety of young guests.)

By age eight, most kids have outgrown their child-size table and chairs, so if you haven't put a desk and work chair in the room, it's probably time. Even if your child does most homework at the kitchen table or in the family room, he or

FUN WITH FABRIC

With the limitless selection of fabrics available on the market today, it's easy to understand why so many designers turn to this medium when they need an inexpensive way to dress up a room. Fabric is especially suitable in children's rooms because it can be cleaned (make sure it's machine washable before purchasing to save money on dry cleaning). Here are some clever ways to freshen a child's room with fabric.

No-Sew Slipcovers

Instead of investing in custom-sewn covers, make your own by draping a large piece of fabric over a chair and tucking it underneath cushions and around sides. For a finishing touch, hot-glue decorative braid or fringe around the unfinished edge of the fabric. This also works well for a headboard. A bonus? These slipcovers can be easily removed for washing.

Pillow Talk

It's amazing how something as simple as a pillow can completely change the look of a room. For a splash of color, make a variety of throw pillows and floor cushions in your child's favorite solid colors and interesting patterns. Embellish them with juvenile trims and buttons. If you can't sew, simply lay a pillow form in the center of a large fabric square, then knot the diagonal fabric corners together across the pillow.

Scrappy Idea

A plain strip of fabric works wonders when wrapped around curtain rods, lamp bases, or chandelier cords. It's also a novel way to use up scraps of fabric and an inexpensive solution for hiding lamp bases and curtain rods in dated colors and styles. For best results, cut the fabric on the bias, at least 1½ feet wide and as long as desired. Use glue to secure end of fabric to item you are wrapping, then wrap fabric around item, overlapping the edges. Ribbons will produce the same effect.

Cushion Comfort

Add personality to plain bar stools and ordinary chairs with delightful cushion covers. There's no need to spend a lot of money to have them recovered when it's so simple to make your own. For round cushions, cut a circle from fabric, about 6 inches larger in diameter than the cushion. Stitch elastic or fuse a casing around edges, then fit cover around cushion. For a square cushion, cut a fabric square 8 inches larger than cushion. Lay fabric on cushion top, then tie corners together over the bottom of the cushion.

Clever Cover-ups

Create additional storage space with fabric skirts. Glue 1 side of a Velcro hook and loop fastener around the edge of a table and the other side around the top edge of a piece of fabric. When you put the two together, you have a clever skirt that hides whatever you store underneath. You can do the same with an old box. By skirting the sides and painting the top to match the fabric, you can make an attractive end table or nightstand in no time.

Fabric Art

Instead of purchasing expensive art, stretch an interesting piece of fabric over a wood frame and hang it on a wall. Make it as big or as small as you like.

Wonders for Walls

Fabric isn't just for furniture anymore. You can also cover walls with wonderful fabric textures and patterns. Apply fabric in the same manner as wallpaper, or staple it to tops of walls and then cover staples with a strip of wood molding or cording. Or, simply turn fabric edges under and tack them to wall with decorative upholstery tacks. Another quick wall cover is to sheer a length of fabric onto curtain rods, then hang rods at top and bottom of walls.

Screen Scene

Add extra storage to an empty corner or separate a room into distinct areas with decorative fabric screens. All you have to do is buy the frames and then insert whatever fabric you want. It's a decorating element that never goes out of style, simply because you can change the fabric to suit current decorating trends.

Super Shades

Roller blinds have a clean, crisp look that provides both light and privacy, and the do-it-yourself kits are quite inexpensive. Buy a kit that will fit your window's measurements, then, using the fabrics in your room as a guide, purchase a lightweight fabric like cotton and cut it to fit the size of the shade. Apply fusible webbing to wrong side of fabric, fuse fabric to front of shade, and voilà! You have a custom-designed roller blind that complements the look of your room.

Easy-to-Clean Laminates

Sticky fingers and dirty paws can often ruin fabrics. Instead of chancing it, cover cushion fabrics and table linens with easy-to-clean laminates. Local fabric stores carry iron-on laminates that can be applied to small pieces of fabric, while upholstery shops and decorator fabric stores can send the fabric away to be professionally laminated.

A girl who loves vibrant colors and patterns used calendar pages, posters, and photos to express her personal vision. Bedding in a mix of brilliant yet coordinating prints carries out the energetic, harmonious scheme. Manufacturer: 3M.

cope with premature aches and pains. In addition, good task lighting is essential to prevent eyestrain, so be sure to put a lamp at your child's desk and another at bedside.

Toys of all kinds proliferate more than ever at this age, and, now that the choking danger is past, you can expect to find tiny Lego blocks, Barbie shoes, and other miniature items migrating all over the house. More storage with more cubbyholes, drawers, and compartments really come in handy now, and you can be fairly inventive in your storage solutions. If you want kids to help with picking up, opt for good-looking open storage containers. For clothes as well as toys, systems that require neat stacking and folding may not work as well as those that allow items to be tossed into storage units. You might decide to choose your battles and be satisfied as long as they stash all similar items together—off the floor.

To further clear out the clutter in a grade-schooler's room, kids this age might be willing to part with some of the toys, clothes, and collections from their younger years, but don't be surprised if they are a bit ambivalent. Giving to children in need may inspire some altruistic youngsters, while other kids will get excited if you hold a garage sale and let them keep the money made from their old toys and clothing. If all else fails, you can transfer your children's outgrown items to the attic or the basement for the time being. Remember: The important thing is to make more room for everyday living—kid style.

PERSONAL STYLE STARS: PRETEENS

Children ages nine to 12 are at a crossroads between childhood and the teenage years. Bedroom decor becomes a

she needs a dedicated study spot to stash paperwork and start responsible work habits.

Plan for a student desk and chair—or a full-size desk and a chair that has a seat that can be raised—plus a two-drawer file cabinet or equivalent storage. If your child will be using the computer anywhere in the house, make sure it's on a desktop that allows for comfortable, strain-free use. Kids have enough challenges sticking to a task without having to

To a teen, cool is important, but so is warmth. Natural wood in a contemporary style delivers both beautifully. Keep the calm look going with neutral backgrounds, or add excitement with vivid hues. Real wood looks great either way. Retailer: Gautier USA, Inc.

major means of self-expression at the same time it becomes a significant way to gain peer approval. While toys are still important, hobbies, collections, electronic equipment, music, and clothes are much more so. Storage for all these items can be a challenge, but they can provide a basis for decorating, too.

Preteens and teens tend to want a real hand in decorating their rooms, so encourage them to express their individuality with displays of equipment, trophies, and decorative motifs that symbolize their accomplishments and interests. Just be sure to leave room for the usual celebrity posters and memorabilia, too. One of the best gifts for a child this age is a large (22×26-inch or more) cork bulletin board, stylishly framed and covered in a kid-friendly fabric. Depending on your child's tastes, fabric depicting everything from rainbows to race cars can be used to cover a corkboard. For a more ageless, chic look, consider a leopard or zebra skin print, jewel-tone stripes, or another funky pattern that works with the room's color scheme.

At this age, bunk beds and other childish structures will probably fall out of favor. A bunk bed set that can be converted into two twin beds or a daybed that has a studio apartment look will probably meet their needs better. Girls may want a dressing table, student desks may be outgrown, and the open-bin storage units from earlier days may no longer handle the job.

If you've already purchased furniture with an eye to the future, a classic twin bed or a daybed with a trundle will do just fine. If not, now may be the time to buy a full-size (double) bed or a more grown-up–looking twin bed. Dressers and chests of drawers gain new importance as do hutches or bookcases with open shelving to display trophies and other treasures.

A full-size desk and an adjustable-height desk chair are essential now, as many preteens start preferring to do homework in their rooms. At this age, unsupervised Internet use can pose a danger, but a computer is likely to be a school-work necessity. You may want to designate your child's bedroom desk as the spot for paperwork and simple project typing and leave the Internet-connected computer in the family room. Wherever they work, kids of all ages need good task lighting positioned so that there is ample illumination on pages but no glare on the computer screen.

Preteens don't play on the floor much any more, but they still love to lounge there. If you've got the "no messy snacks in the bedroom" rule down pat, you may want to indulge your youngster in a new carpet now. New rug or not, a few big colorful floor pillows will be an instant hit with the after-school and sleepover crowd.

Most kids at this age are much more interested in clothes than ever before, but, unfortunately, they are seldom more interested in taking care of them. Plenty of drawers and cubbyholes or shelves can make it worth their while to be neater: With everything visible, it's easier and faster to put together outfits on those rushed school mornings. Hooks or pegs will still work better than hangers, but you can start making the switch now by offering some of each.

TEENS: TAKING ON THE WORLD

If you didn't redecorate your youngster's room during the preteen stage, you will probably want to do so now. Ideally, you and your teen can work together to create a look you're both happy with and one that can last awhile. For starters, new wall paint and a new bed ensemble can be had on most budgets. If the room needs adult-size furniture, good quality hand-me-downs can enjoy a new lease on life with custom refinishing. A computer armoire or a desk/hutch may be the only "new" pieces really needed; if so, ready-to-finish furniture stores offer pieces you can finish to coordinate with existing furniture pieces.

If your teen is the responsible type, new carpeting or area rugs also may be worthwhile now. For practicality's sake, you'll still want to skip the pastel velvety carpets in favor of a more robust variety in a tweedy midtone hue. Oriental-style rugs, with their jewel-tone patterns, give an opulent grown-up look and hide spills, too. For another adult touch, replace floor cushions and beanbag chairs with a small easy chair for a guest. The more the room looks like a hip studio apartment, the better most teens will like it. Not coincidentally, this approach will let the room do double duty throughout the college years, too.

Aside from a dramatic-looking bed, the best investment you can make for your teen, if the budget allows, is a professional closet-organizing system. A walk-in closet is a dream come true for most girls and many boys, but even if the closet is small, a professional system can make the very most of the space. If a closet consultant is outside the budget, check out the do-it-yourself racking and stacking systems available through home storage and organization specialty retailers.

Large framed cork bulletin boards corral posters and other teen treasures; if you provided bulletin boards for your preteen, you may want to change the cover fabric and add an extra board or two. Teens have many of the same hobbies as preteens, but by now, they've also got serious levels of homework and lots of post-high school planning to do. Make it easy for them to build their futures from a safe place, right at home.

Building Blocks of Design

Safety has to be your top consideration when shopping for any element of a child's room. Beyond that, you have a wealth of delightful choices in furnishing and decorating a room that's (almost) as special as your child. First, plan for function—the basic things your child will need to do in the room. Then, choose background treatments, furniture, fabrics, and accessories with decorating power to spare. A strong vision will keep your effort on track; a flexible approach will keep the effort creative, cost-effective, and fun for you and your child.

For color confidence, choose two or three hues your child likes, and stick with them (plus shades and tints of the chosen colors) throughout the room. Kids' everyday clutter will introduce enough other colors and patterns, so corralling your scheme will create a calm base.

SAFETY FIRST

If you're lucky enough to have an unlimited budget to spend on an ideal kid's room, feel free to create a fantasy environment from top to bottom. Regardless of how generous your budget may be, however, be sure to put safe, sturdy construction—the surest test of quality—at the top of your must-have list. Even theatrical set construction needs both a designer and a technical director who make sure the design is constructed for the actors' safety, so make sure your little star gets the same consideration.

One of the most difficult challenges a new parent faces is to anticipate all of the ways a child can get hurt. Kids and adults think differently, and what looks innocuous to you can be dangerous to them—and in just a second or two. In many metropolitan areas, you can hire a company to come in and childproof your home, but you can also do the job yourself. Consult the U.S. Consumer Products Safety Commission for guidelines on crib bars, bunk beds, and many other children's products, or look for the commission's label of approval on products you buy. The Juvenile Products Manufacturers Association also certifies merchandise for safety and labels those that meet the industry's voluntary standards. Following are some of the basics for safety.

Cute and cozy, this red-and-white room is just right for a little one. The crib is far enough away from the miniblind cord, and the crib has locking sides to prevent falls. Just be sure to take out the decorative pillows when it's naptime or bedtime. Designer: Lyn Peterson. Wallpaper: Motif Designs.

BEDS AND CRIBS

- If your kids are set on bunk beds, be sure to keep children under seven off the top bunk and insist on safety rails and a safety ladder regardless of kids' ages.
- Make sure bunk beds are sturdy. Check to ensure spacing of rails are too narrow for a child's head to get caught.
- Choose bunk beds with guardrails on both sides of the top bunk so you can relocate the bed if needed. Make sure the top bunk's mattress is at least five inches below the edge of the guardrails.
- Buy only cribs with slats/bars too close together for a baby's head to get caught. Slats must measure no more than two and one-eighth inches apart, and corner posts should be no more than one-sixteenth of an inch high (exception: canopy posts and other posts taller than 16 inches). Decorative cutouts on cribs and beds should be too small for any part

of a child's body to get caught. You will need to add extra slats to make that charming antique crib (or most cribs made before 1990) safe.

- Make sure latching mechanisms that let you lower a crib side are securely latched in the highest position unless you're lifting out the baby. Choose a crib with this mechanism out of baby's reach or one that needs ten pounds of pressure for release.
- Buy the sturdiest crib you can afford. Your baby will do a lot of jumping and jouncing before he or she outgrows the crib.

CHANGING TABLES

- Use a changing table with a low guardrail and a safety strap.
- Keep diapering supplies and extra clothes in open storage at arm's reach of the changing table so you don't have to leave the child unattended on the table, even for a moment.

ELECTRIC AND HEAT

- Keep electrical cords out of the way to keep kids from grabbing them or tripping on them, and rearrange furniture if necessary to eliminate extension cords.
- Screen off any radiator or other heat source so children can't bump or fall into it.
- Make sure all electrical outlets are equipped with ground fault circuit interrupters, and block unused outlets with the simple plastic safety caps available at most hardware and grocery stores.

FIREARMS

- If you own a firearm, keep it unloaded and locked away, and store ammunition separately. Statistically, far more family members and neighbors' kids than intruders are hurt or killed by guns in the home.

FURNITURE AND ACCESSORIES

- Bolt bookcases or wall unit pieces to a wall to keep heavy pieces from falling if a child climbs them.
- Make sure toy chests have a closing mechanism that keeps them from slamming down on fingers. (If you're using an antique hope chest for toy storage, have a safety hinge retrofitted and remove the hinge on the front lock.)
- You probably already know to avoid decorative accessories and accents with small parts that pose a choking hazard for babies, toddlers, and preschoolers. If you want to use beads, ball fringe, or other small elements that can be detached (or yanked off), confine them to rooms small children will not use. If a room is shared between a preschooler and an older child, keep the potential problem items up high on a wall-mounted shelf or otherwise out of reach.
- Position storage hooks—and anything else with the potential to poke—at a level that's either below or above your child's eyes.

KITCHENS AND BATHS

- If you're buying a cooktop or range, get one with controls on top or in back—not down on the front where young kids can reach them.
- Avoid sharp edges and corners anywhere children will have access. Round or oval tables throughout the house and rounded or bullnose kitchen and bath countertops provide safety without compromising adult style.
- Install simple plastic kiddie locks on all cabinets kids can reach (including the ones they can reach by climbing on a chair and standing on the counter when you're in the next room). Be especially vigilant about locking cabinets holding cleaning supplies, medicines, matches, saws, knives, and other potentially dangerous kitchen and craft tools.

- Station a mirror in the bath where small children can see themselves to reduce the temptation to climb up on the counter for a look.
- Use only bath rugs with nonslip backings (or use a cut-to-fit nonslip pad available separately). If you're having new flooring installed, specify tile with a nonslip surface.
- Have grab bars installed in the tub and near the toilet, and tell kids not to hang on towel bars or put weight on them. (Grab bars must be reinforced with a block spanning two wall studs, so plan for them if you are rehabbing or building new.)
- Install antiscald devices on your bathroom faucets, especially in showers and bathtubs. Children's skin is much thinner than adults', and it can burn severely in just a few seconds.

PAINTS AND STAINS

- Choose low-VOC latex paints rather than oilbase paints for kids' rooms; they emit less fumes and are less toxic.
- When it comes to finishing wood floors in kids' rooms, a waterbase urethane is less toxic and less flammable than polyurethane.

SMOKE ALARMS

- Install at least one smoke alarm on every level of your home, and add a carbon monoxide detector near bedrooms if you use gas or oil heat or have an attached garage. Change batteries in your detectors on the same date every year, such as Thanksgiving, a birthday, or the autumn return to standard time.

STAIRS

- Install safety gates to keep children away from stairs. If stair railings or landing balusters are more than five inches apart, install a mesh safety barrier.

At the end of the day (or any other time), comfort comes down to a cozy place for a cuddle in loving adult arms. A chair that glides or rocks recalls the prenatal rocking motion that means safety at its most elemental level. Upholstered arms and a footrest give a weary parent a chance to relax, too. Designer: Karen Cashman, Perspectives.

WINDOWS

- For second-story windows, install window guards instead of relying on screens or storm windows. If your windows are double hung, simple devices can be put in place to keep the window from opening more than a few inches while still allowing for easy operation by an adult in case of fire.
- Secure window blind cords up high, and keep other dangling items away from where a child can reach them.

There's no way you can completely childproof any environment, so do yourself and your kids a favor and teach them that "no" means "no." They'll comply to win your approval years before they understand safety issues.

COMFORT, INSIDE AND OUT

Physical comfort in your child's room comes down to a few commonsense elements. The shortlist is a bed with a good-quality, supportive mattress (you'll go through at least two mattresses before he or she heads for college); enough storage drawers and ones that move easily; round pegs at the right height for hanging clothes; adequate lighting for tasks; and a good-size work surface plus supportive chair. If you don't have a home security system, make sure bedroom win-dows have high-quality locks and, if you like a little fresh air, window guards that let windows open no more than five inches.

Psychological comfort is just as important, so plan that in from the start. Starting at the most elemental level, nights can feel endless to a child who's ill or even just one with a healthy imagination. An extra bed in the room will be more comfortable for everyone when you're on the parental night shift, and a rocking chair can save your back as well as soothe a fretful youngster. If a conventional twin bed won't work well, consider a futon-type couch, a daybed with a pullout trundle bed, or an armchair that converts to a twin sleeper.

Red, blue, and yellow, the primary colors from which all other hues are made, give a young, cheerful, straight-forward feeling that's just right for a young boy's room. White plus natural wood tones make a soothing background for these vivid flag colors. Manufacturer: Village, A Brand of FSC Wallcoverings.

A night-light is important, but you and your child may prefer a conventional lamp with a dim (15-watt) bulb or a dimmer switch instead of the usual tiny plug-ins. (In any case, be sure the shade isn't too close to the bulb.) Of all the bedroom accessories, your child will find a treasured blanket or a special stuffed animal a bedtime must: This is one item you shouldn't feel in a rush to remove. For kids over age five, a small unbreakable flashlight may also help them feel in control and comforted. Night fears come and go as children's brains develop; most outgrow them as preadolescents if not before. Security in early years has lifetime benefits, and, while nothing can take the place of a comforting adult, a room designed to make a child feel more secure can make a difference.

HAVE FUN WITH COLOR

Everything you need to know about decorating with color you didn't learn in kindergarten! However, the job of choosing and using colors can be fun and even easy. It's worthwhile, too, because color is the most emotional and compelling element in any setting.

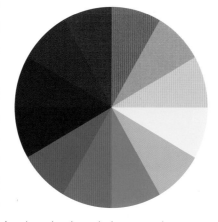

A color wheel can help you and your child choose a color scheme, whether it's a traditional primary grouping or something a bit more adventurous, such as orange, blue-violet, and white or black.

To understand color basics and "what goes with what" most reliably, picture a circle cut into 12 sections like in a pie. Colors are arranged around this circle in the order of a rainbow: red, red-orange, orange, yellow-orange, yellow, yellow-green, green, blue-green, blue, blue-violet, violet, and red-violet.

Some of the approaches interior designers use to cook up color schemes are easy to do with a color wheel. (Find one at craft and art stores or make your own.) A complementary scheme pairs two colors opposite each other on the color wheel; for example, orange and blue or red-orange and blue-green. A split complementary uses two colors on each side of a color's complement; for example, orange plus blue-green and blue-violet.

Even easier, use an analogous scheme of three colors that are side by side on the color wheel. Blue-violet, blue, and blue-green make a wonderfully cool, restful setting, while yellow-orange, yellow, and yellow-green are energetic and cheerful.

Remember, you can extend any color with the neutrals: white, beige, brown, gray, and black. A favorite color that may seem overwhelming on its own is very manageable when surrounded by neutrals. Red, white, and black; orange, beige, and brown; and purple, white, and gray are three proven examples.

It's much easier to see your options when you use a color wheel, but if you can't find one at your local craft store, use colored pencils or paint chips to try out various combinations until you get one your child likes. However, if you find this too complex to fuss with, don't worry. Look at printed fabrics or wallcoverings at your local store for well-designed color schemes already available. You don't have to buy the fabric or paper, just pick up the color scheme. Be sure to use the colors in the same proportion as you see them on the fabric or wallpaper. In general, the most livable schemes use a light or cool color in the largest amount, a medium color in the next largest amount, and the brightest, most intense or dark color in the smallest amount (as an accent). Avoid visual chaos by keeping the basic scheme to two or three colors, and add variety by using shades and tints of these colors plus neutrals. When you get all the clothes, souvenirs, toys, and other paraphernalia of the typical child (or two) in that room, things will be plenty colorful!

WINNING THE PRIMARIES

Red, blue, and yellow are the three primary colors because they can't be created by mixing other colors. You can stop right here for some kids and use these three colors, or any two of them, with foolproof success. White, black, or wood-tone furniture all count as neutral colors that don't compete with your main hues. And, after all, what's more classic than red, white, and blue (great with Early American, French country, or modern furnishings) or more refreshing than blue, yellow, and white (perfect with Swedish country, contemporary, and beach cottage styles). To lighten up the primary colors to baby blue, pink, and pale lemon, just add white.

SUCCESS WITH SECONDARY COLORS

In between the primary colors are the three secondary colors made from mixing two primary colors together. Orange (mix of red and yellow), green (yellow plus blue), and purple or violet (blue plus red), expand your choices. While it's possible to use true blue and Kelly green or

red and orange together, you may want to start out with a less demanding combination. Here are a few popular choices you might offer for your kids' approval:

• Green and yellow—fresh as a sunny meadow. Add orange accents for punch.

Green and violet, two secondary colors, look pretty with yellow and blue, two primary colors. Together, they create a summer garden feeling that is fun and frisky as well as feminine. Note that a dark shade and a light tint of violet "count" as one color, expanding your decorating options. Retailer: JCPMedia L.P.

This split complementary color scheme blends yellow and yellow-green, two analogous (side-by-side) colors, then contrasts them with violet, yellow's complement. Backed up by lots of pristine white, the result is fresh, cool, and springlike. Manufacturer: Waverly.

- Red, yellow, and green—cheerful as a circus or a field of tulips. Lighten the red to pink for a fun flower garden scheme of pink, green, and yellow. Even simpler, use just pink and green.
- Orange and blue—a favorite of boys. Add white to the orange for a soft, peachy tint that appeals to girls, too.

While orange appeals immediately and green is soothing and popular, you may find purple a bit somber for very young children—unless, of course, it comes packaged as a friendly dinosaur. To put purple in the picture more easily, try one of these:

- Regal purple and cheerful golden yellow—ideal for a knightly setting.
- Lilac (purple plus white) and spring green—a scheme that's both chic and as charming as a garden.
- Purple and pink—a little girl's favorite.
- Lilac, yellow, and green—sprightly as springtime.

Tickle Them with Tertiary Colors

Tertiary (third-level) colors are made from mixing two secondary colors or a primary and a secondary color. The six tertiary colors—red-orange, yellow-orange, yellow-green, blue-green, blue-violet, and red-violet—give you the full range of color-scheming options. Lighten them with white for watercolor effects, or use them with black or gray for drama that will captivate a hard-to-please teen. Here are a few combinations to consider:

- Yellow-green (also known as lime), purple (or lilac), and black
- Blue-green (aqua, turquoise, teal), red-orange (coral), and yellow-orange plus white or black
- Red, blue-violet, and gray
- Blue-violet, red-violet, and yellow-green
- Orange, blue-violet (or periwinkle), and white or black

Working with Kids' Color Preferences

You want to indulge your child's color preferences, but you cringe at the thought of midnight black or construction orange all over the walls. You don't have to go to those extremes to create a room your child will love. The secret is diluting the over-the-top color, either literally with white paint or visually by surrounding it with more temperate tones.

Young children often adore bright red and orange; girls in particular may crave hot pink and bright orchid purple. Let them enjoy these happy hues in a way that doesn't overwhelm the room by using one or more cooling strategies.

A glacial scheme of gray and white would look too cold, but not when you add strategic hits of warm orange and natural green. Repeat a color in at least three places around the room for visual balance. Retailer: Gautier USA, Inc.

Try adding white or beige to orange to make this lively hue more versatile. Boys and girls alike will feel at home with warm terra-cotta and melon hues; for more interest, add a bit of yellow or red to create sunflower or coral. These sunset tones work well with Wild West motifs and many other decorating themes. Easily coordinating colors include blues, greens, yellows, rust red, and warm neutral colors such as cream, tan, and brown. Peach plus lilac or periwinkle makes a pretty, chic look.

To keep classic red from being too much of a good thing, use it as an accent throughout the room, and find a predominantly red bed ensemble to make the bed the center of attention. Popular color schemes are red, white, and royal blue; red, pale gray, and violet; red, yellow, and turquoise; red, white, and green (lime is fresh, hunter is classic); or red, white, and pink. Let white and cool colors (blue, green, violet) dominate, and keep the hot colors (red, yellow, pink) as accents since they'll just naturally grab more attention.

It looks bright but doesn't feel jarring—proof that this color scheme is actually very clever. Yellow-green, yellow, and yellow-orange make one harmonious blend; red, orchid pink, and blue make another; and the two blends complement each other with pizzazz.

hard to paint over later. (They don't do a lot for the depression a lot of teens feel now and then either.) You can keep deep-tone drama without the dreariness, however. If your teen likes black, paint the walls ice blue, light acid green, or another hip, light tint, and furnish the room with black lacquer or black metal furniture, available in many styles and price points. Bed linen ensembles featuring prints in black plus neon hues are easy to come by and deliver drama aplenty.

The same principle applies to deep tones of purple or any other dark or intensely vivid color that might be overwhelming to live with. A young man who likes the drama of purple might find light gray walls and gunmetal gray furniture a cool background for the regal color, while a young lady might enjoy a scheme using lilac or lime plus white, accented by full-strength purple accessories.

Try to keep the backgrounds and large furniture pieces simple and classic for long-term comfort. Accessories, from accent pillows to bulletin boards and picture frames, can be changed as often as youngster's

Bright pink and purple are so popular with young girls that it's easy to find ensembles and accents that pair these two. To keep them from overwhelming the room, choose a pale pink, lilac, or periwinkle tint for walls, and cool the look further with lots of white and light green. (Lime is fresh; mint is timeless.) If your girl likes a vintage look, it's easy to find elements in old rose, lavender, ivory, and celadon or sage green.

Many preteens and teens crave dark colors, but somber hues tend to overwhelm an average-size room and can be

tastes do. If your daughter's taste has changed from pastel pink to fire engine red, do both of you a favor and drop doting family members a hint before her birthday or the holidays. Accessory items make perfect gifts and will let her change more often or make more of a statement, economically.

By the time your children have a more-than-sporadic interest in decorating their rooms, they're ready to start grasping the idea of buying what furthers the look not just what catches their eye. Impulsive shoppers as well as those who vacillate endlessly (you may have both in one household) will find it easier and more fun to purchase things that "go with" a turquoise ocean-inspired theme or a green-and-brown Wild West theme. Vacation trips, birthdays, and other special events all offer opportunities to help kids create environments that reflect their interests and dreams.

PATTERN PERFECT

If you're looking for a pattern to energize your child's room, you don't have to look very far. Stripes (circus, racing, or candy) are always popular, and not just with kids. You can find a striped fabric or wallcovering in just about any colors you like, or paint a scheme on walls yourself. Keep in mind that horizontal stripes tend to make walls look wider: For a room that resembles a bowling alley, visually widen the narrow end walls with horizontal stripes. Use vertical stripes to visually raise the typical eight-foot ceiling. Don't have too much contrast; yellow and black stripes, for instance, will tend to visually "vibrate" in a stressful way.

Plaid is another timeless favorite that looks handsome in jewel tones (ruby, emerald, sapphire, etc.). It can also look pretty but sporty in hot pastel tints. Plaid's squared-off shapes give it a tailored look, but the blending of color tones can add warmth and interest to any decor. Plaid's simpler cousin, checks, shares a lot of the same charm. Color makes all the difference: Imagine pretty pink-and-white gingham checks in a countrified nursery or no-nonsense navy-and-ivory checks in a collegiate room.

Florals are timeless feminine favorites, but today's girl may not like the nostalgic approach of yore. The antidote: contemporary freehand florals mixed with stripes or checks, all done up in fresh paintbox colors. Manufacturer: PJ Kids.

A jungle theme takes naturally to the climbing fun of bunk beds in this charming room with appeal for boys and girls alike. Rounded posts are attractive as well as safe for active young explorers. Manufacturer: Waverly.

Flower prints don't have the unisex versatility of geometric stripes, plaids, and checks, but in a girl's room, you can combine geometric patterns and freeform florals for prettiness with punch. If you want botanical motifs in a boy's room, consider geometric, stylized Arts and Crafts–style florals or simple greenery, from ivy borders to palm tree murals.

Wallcovering borders and stencils expand your choice of appealing pattern motifs. Today's laser-cut borders feature a great array of sport, animal, fairy-tale, and cartoon motifs. In most cases, coordinating wallcoverings and easy-care fabrics

are also available. If you're not sure your child's current enthusiasm will last, paint the walls and use just the easily strippable wallcovering border from a popular set.

Thanks to today's aggressive marketing of line extensions, it's easy to find themed accessories from many TV shows and movies marketed to kids. Look at your child's favorite next time with an eye to determining the color and pattern schemes. They're usually very pronounced for easy recognition by mini consumers. For example, Disney's *The Lion King* used African basket-inspired zigzag patterns in gold, rust, and black; the essence of *101 Dalmatians* was conveyed with black-and-white polka dots plus a bit of red for emphasis; and *The Little Mermaid* is swirling waves of aqua with accents of coral.

You get the idea. Once you have the main colors and patterns figured out, you can create the impression your child craves in a way that won't be dated in three months. After all, the patterns of animal skins, shells, flowers, leaves, and other natural elements have been captivating people since long before modern media were around.

TOP PRIORITY: A GOOD BED AND MATTRESS

Just as designers advise you to spend the bulk of your living room budget on quality upholstered pieces, you'll want to spend more on the all-important bed than on storage or accessory pieces.

CRADLE COMFORT

For the first several years, a baby sleeps a lot of the time, so a cozy, comfortable, and safe bed is just as important for these little ones as for older kids and adults. Many parents skip bassinets or cradles because babies outgrow them in just a few months, after which they're unsafe. If you must have a cradle, choose one with the highest sides possible, and make sure the rocking motion is slight so baby can't fall out. A model that lets you lock the cradle into a nonswinging position is ideal. If you like a bassinet, make sure it has a stable base to avoid tipping over. While they won't stay in a crib for more than a few years, you'll want to buy one that's sturdy, with smooth, snag-free surfaces and safely rounded corners. You'll also want to be sure the crib's slats or bars are close enough together to prevent the baby from getting his or her head caught. Many old cribs have bars too far apart, so if you're using an heirloom hand-me-down, be sure to retrofit it with extra bars.

If the crib's sides can be raised and lowered, be sure the locking mechanism that keeps the side up works well, and remind everyone to use it faithfully. (Babies don't always tell you when they're ready to make a grab for support in an attempt to stand up, and you don't want the crib side to let them down.)

GROWING UP AND OUT

When your child is ready to leave the crib, usually around age two, you can invest in an interim toddler bed that's low to the ground, but you don't need to. A simple bed frame or even a mattress and box spring set directly on the floor will do the job nicely for the couple of years it's needed.

When your child is up and running, a sturdy bed and a good-quality mattress and box spring will give a growing body the support it needs to rest comfortably—and will also survive the occasional "monkeys jumping on the bed." Experts advise replacing mattresses at least every ten years, so if you have to choose between a supportive new mattress/box spring and a new bed frame, choose the former. You can always repaint or refinish the frame, but even the old board in the bed trick will not really improve a less-than-supportive mattress.

Good mattresses and box springs are always on sale somewhere, so plan ahead to get the best price on this essential. Always use a box spring with the mattress; the box spring supports the mattress so it can support your little dreamer. (For health reasons, don't use hand-me-down mattresses, and think twice about taking other upholstered pieces. However, old quilts, linens, and other fabric items that can be washed are fine.)

When you go mattress shopping, take your youngster along so he or she can "test rest" several mattresses in the price range you've selected. While innerspring mattresses are generally the most supportive and popular at all price points, you may be interested in foam, air, or even flotation (once known as waterbed) options. If you are considering foam, make sure it's supportive enough, and plan to use a coordinating electric heater with any flotation system. If you're considering an innerspring mattress, remember that "firm" doesn't have to feel hard thanks to today's pillow-top cushioning. Every body is different, so let your child try out several choices. A mattress used every day for a decade should be one your child will find comfortable from the start.

When your child is about five years old and demanding a "big kid's bed," you'll have a wealth of choices to work with. Most kids adore bunk beds, and they do save space if the room is shared, but make sure you can keep little ones off the top bunk. Also be sure bunk beds have guardrails and that mattresses are five inches or more below these guardrails; even big kids can roll out of bed while asleep. A safety ladder is another must-have. Bunk beds have undergone rigorous legislation in recent years, so look for those labeled as being in compliance with safety laws and industry standards. Many kids decide, as they enter their teens, that they're too old for bunk beds, so it's also wise to choose bunks that can be uncoupled and used as twin beds.

If bunk beds aren't your child's style but you're short on space, consider a loft bed. These feature elevated beds with a play area underneath or a desk and other storage. Some offer a second twin bed that installs under the loft. Loft beds work best in bedrooms with ceilings of more than eight feet.

Another space saver is a low-profile trundle bed, available in styles from contemporary to traditional. One twin bed unit pulls out from underneath another to accommodate a sleepover guest. Some trundles are freestanding units on casters that are stowed under the primary bed and easily roll out when an extra bed is needed. Other styles sit on frames attached to the primary bed; these also roll out from under the bed. Choose a trundle that moves smoothly and easily and is one your child can handle alone, and be sure corners on the lower bed's frame aren't sharp.

Similar to a trundle bed, a captain's bed is a twin bed with a number of storage drawers beneath, all on the same frame. Some beds have both a second trundle bed and built-in drawers. A captain's bed that is authentically styled has high sides to keep the sleeper from "going overboard."

Inspired by classic Swedish built-in beds and colored in romantic ice pink and celery, this fairy-tale room is sophisticated and timeless as well as pretty. The real beauty is the multitude of built-in under-the-bed drawers that eliminate the need for a bulky dresser. Designer: Jeanne Benner, Benner Interiors.

Canopy beds are a traditional style that, in twin sizes, are marketed mostly to girls. The beds' tall posts support a framework that can support a fabric covering. Some come with drawers or a trundle below. A variant with some of a canopy bed's drama but that may appeal to both boys and girls is a bed with tall pencil posts but no canopy.

A twin-size bed is adequate, but, if the bedroom is spacious enough to accommodate it, consider using a full-size bed (also called a double). Once the standard for couples, the full/double bed has been replaced in most master bedrooms by a queen- or king-size model. Following this trend toward "supersizing," an older child may be more comfortable in a double bed than in a twin.

BEDDING

Bedding is one way you can create a big, trendy statement in a child's room without breaking the bank. Even a twin bed takes up a good amount of the space in a typical bedroom, so you don't have to do much more than replace bed linens to give the room a whole new look.

Novelty "bed in a bag" ensembles include a comforter, bed skirt, and pillow shams as well as sheets and pillow-

STORAGE SOLUTIONS

Inherent treasure hunters, children covet each new find with enthusiasm and wonder. In children's rooms, however, assorted collections often vie for the same space as socks, books, and shirts. To stretch storage and display space in the bedroom, try these handy suggestions.

- Clip hair bows on a **ribbon hanger.** To make your own, fold the end of a 1½-inch-wide grosgrain ribbon (about 36 inches long) over the bottom of a wire hanger. Staple in place. Clip hair bows to ribbon, and hang in closet.
- Toys, art supplies, or seasonal clothes can be conveniently stored **under the bed** and hidden by a dust ruffle. Purchase plastic bins, or cut large, heavy cardboard boxes down to size. Spray paint them in colors to match the room's decor.
- Stack neatly folded blankets and quilts **atop armoires.**
- Install rows of **wooden pegs** at heights reachable by little arms. These are great for hats, coats, necklaces, and other items that benefit from hanging.
- Group videos, CDs, games, doll clothes, and blocks in **sturdy baskets** that fit on shelves and inside armoires. These baskets hide clutter yet provide easy storage for hard-to-stash items. Likewise, large wicker baskets are ideal for catching balls and sports equipment. Note: If you use matching baskets or bins, the clutter looks neater and more organized.
- Stretch **fishnet** over a corner to catch stuffed animals and dolls.
- Decorative molding doubles as **picture displays.** Have a piece of molding and a piece of quarter round cut to desired length. Tack quarter round to top edge of molding to form a lip. Paint as desired. When molding is hung on wall, quarter round will keep picture frames from slipping.
- Need extra space for books or stuffed animals? Mount a **bracketed shelf** on the top of a windowsill.
- Freestanding **coatracks** are catchalls for coats, school bags, and robes.
- Make an **art portfolio** by folding a piece of poster board in half and stapling along 2 sides. Collect your child's artwork inside, sliding portfolio behind a dresser or chest when not in use. At the end of the school year, you'll have all the artwork together so you can sort through and keep the best.
- Clean out **aluminum cans** in various sizes; tape or file any sharp edges and remove labels. Place on a windowsill or desk to collect pencils, markers—even combs and hairbrushes.
- In closets, **bookcases** or **wood cubbies** stacked against an empty wall or pushed underneath hanging clothes make good storage for shoes, sweaters, and books.
- Make a **display rack** by tacking or hot gluing clothespins or metal clamps to a painted yardstick. Affix yardstick to wall, and use to display family photos and artwork. Another clever option is to stretch heavy string or wire across a wall. Use painted clothespins to hang art and photos on the string or wire.
- Catch dirty clothes by making **laundry bags** out of pillowcases. Just run heavy rope through the hem of a pillowcase, then hang bag in a closet. You may want to use different pillowcases so clothes can be sorted for laundering.

Pink, deep rose, and green with yellow accents make a sprightly garden-inspired room for a young lady of any age. Lavish floral appliqués and small flower accents fulfill the garden-pretty theme. Whimsical prints are available that will pick up virtually any motif your child loves.

If you prefer something a bit more subtle, tame the latest cartoon- or movie-theme novelty sheets and pillowcases with a comforter, shams, bed skirt, and window treatments in solid colors that coordinate with the sheet's colors. When the bed is opened at night, the favorite scheme is a fun surprise. The catch here is to make sure your child likes the colors used in the novelty print as well as the characters depicted.

If you'd rather stick to bedding with more staying power, choose a whimsical print designed to delight youngsters beyond the next holiday movie release. Tropical fish, lizards, cats, stripes, flowers, gingham checks, and scores of other colorful choices abound, many with solid color comforters and other coordinates.

Whatever you and your child choose, don't let a novelty print overwhelm the whole room. Merchandising photos aside, it's distinctly possible to have too much of even a good thing. Focus the eye-catching print on one or two areas, and use solid colors or simple patterns on the rest of the room. Keep in mind that kids' belongings will always increase the visual clutter quotient—a lot—so keep backgrounds on the calmer side.

STORAGE FURNITURE: A PLACE FOR EVERYTHING

When it comes to storing the multitude of things kids accumulate, "easier" usually translates into "neater." Especially when they're younger, open compartments—and lots of them—suit many kids better than closed drawers, cupboards, and closets.

If getting your kids to hang up clothes and equipment is next to impossible, skip hard-to-handle hangers in favor of old-fashioned hooks or pegs. One easy way to create a structure for flexible storage is to mount a four-inch-wide molding at chair-rail level around the perimeter of the room. Paint it a color that coordinates with the room's decor, and mount

cases. Some designs are also offered in matching or coordinating throw pillows, window curtains, and table rounds (the tablecloths used to drape small, round tables used as nightstands). Usually economical, these ensembles come decorated with popular cartoon and movie characters almost before a movie hits the video stores. If your child is wild for a particular character or show, you'll be an instant hero if you come home with one of these.

rounded wooden pegs (painted in a contrasting color) at 18-inch intervals. Even inside a closet, install as many hooks or pegs as space allows. In a child's bath, you may want to use more hooks and fewer towel bars. If the bathroom is well-ventilated, towels should dry quickly enough.

The bed itself may yield opportunities for savvy storage. Storage headboards come ready-made, or you can fashion one from small wooden cubicles by linking them together and mounting them a few inches above head level. Under-the-bed storage is great, since kids tend to shove things under there anyway. A captain's bed with built-in drawers in the base of the bed makes a handsome, integrated solution, but you can also buy separate storage drawers on casters to fit under any bed. Depending on how much clearance you have, light-weight plastic storage totes may be a perfectly good solution. If you have access to carpentry skills, build an alcove bed with a shipshape berth on top and storage drawers below.

Stock kitchen cabinets, two-drawer file cabinets, an artist's tabouret (the small rolling carts with lots of little swing-out trays), and a wealth of other nontraditional units make great casual storage in kids' bedrooms and playrooms. Cabinets in wood have a warm look, but metal ones can work just as well in a modern setting. Use appliance paint or other durable enamel to paint metal pieces to match the walls, or choose a cheery color to fit the decorating scheme. A pair of two-drawer file cabinets with a sturdy board on top makes a simple work surface big enough for kids to share. To hide bulky toys or general mess, cover a round table of any size with a floor-length tablecloth, and stash items underneath when necessary. (Other toys can be stashed on top, but don't use a clothed table for a lamp or anything else breakable, as kids often pull on them.)

If you can shave three to five feet or so from one end of a room, set it off with a sheet-turned-curtain suspended from a ceiling-hung rod and turn it into an extra closet for a clothes-loving teen. For easy-access floor storage that's good looking, too, employ canvas-and-wood hampers, wicker hampers, and woven baskets of all kinds. They are just as practical as

Where you have kids you'll have clutter, but it doesn't have to take over their room or their lives. Consider a storage wall that resembles the cubbyhole compartments familiar to preschool kids. There's no easier way to keep everything in its place.

plastic bins and work much better with a traditional or rustic decorating scheme. A toy chest can make a fine storage bench for younger children, but make sure it has a safety hinge and the front lock has been removed.

CHANGING TABLES

A changing table is a must for babies and toddlers. Safety is the prime concern: Choose a changing table that is sturdily constructed and has a safety strap, smoothly rounded corners, and at least a low guardrail to prevent little wrigglers from falling. (Even though you'd never leave a child on a changing table unattended for even a moment, all but the youngest infants have a disconcerting way of moving suddenly, and balance is a foreign concept to them.) Choose a model with one or two lower shelves; it will add to the unit's stability and provide convenient open storage for diapers and baby clothes. Even after he or she is toilet trained, the last child in the household may be willing to use the changing table as display/storage for stuffed animals and other large toys. Some families use a chest of drawers or dresser topped with a waterproof pad as a changing table, but drawers are less convenient than shelves, and the lack of a guardrail can be risky. If you do want to use a conventional dresser as a changing table, retrofit it with simple molding rails available at your local home center or hardware store, and make sure they're smoothly finished.

TOYLAND, TOYLAND

The bigger kids get, the smaller their toys become. Blocks and craft beads in particular seem to slip underfoot with irritating regularity. To keep small toys out of the reach of preschool siblings, stash them in clear plastic shoe boxes on higher shelves. They'll add to the room's colorful ambience and make it easy for kids to find what they want. If a bunch of tiny toys relates to a larger set, such as a model train set or a dollhouse, provide easy-access storage near the main piece. The easier you can make it to put things back where they belong, the fewer struggles you'll have (and the fewer sharp little Barbie shoes or Legos you'll step on at 2 A.M.).

When children start grade school, they'll appreciate furniture and systems that help them avoid losing homework, sports equipment, and personal treasures. Until then, teach children to stash "like with like" by providing as many open or clear-covered boxes, bins, and baskets as they have types of toys. (It's possible to make this task into a sorting game, but you'll have to stay hands-on for longer than you'd like for best results.) Whether you're a Martha Stewart stand-in or very relaxed about clutter, you'll want to enforce the safety aspects of orderliness. At a minimum, even young ones can be taught to keep walkways clear of toys so no one trips, and older children can learn to keep their small toys out of small siblings' reach.

Catalogs and storage specialty stores offer inventive, good-looking solutions of all kinds these days, so make a field trip out of shopping for them with your child. You may not get "buy in" overnight, but he or she will feel part of the process, and that's a start.

NIGHTSTANDS

Once your child is out of the crib or toddler bed, a nightstand of some kind will come in handy to set down a plastic water glass and a bedtime storybook. Rounded corners are preferable, and an extra shelf or drawer is useful, too. If you have a small two-shelf bookcase, small chest, or even a two-drawer file cabinet, you may want to affix a round or oval top made of wood or solid surfacing material. For small children—and big ones who love pillow fights—the nightstand is no place for a table lamp. Choose a wall-mounted lamp instead, and keep the nightstand for unbreakable treasures.

DESKS

These days, homework is a mix of computer and handwritten projects, a situation that is likely to continue for the foreseeable future. Computer desks with drop-down keyboard trays are available in every size and style, so you'll have no problem fitting today's technology into any space and any decorating scheme. Even if you prefer to keep children's computers in safe sight in the family room or home office, you'll want to provide a writing desk of some sort in your child's room.

Younger children will be happy with a table and chair at the right height, and even bigger kids often prefer doing homework at the kitchen or family room table. However, there's nothing like a "real" desk to signal your seriousness about homework, and a desk also makes it easier for kids to keep track of paperwork and reference materials.

For a space-saving desk that's at home in the most traditional settings, computer armoires are attractive and popular solutions for bedroom or family room use. Upper shelves display reference books, and lower drawers store paper and computer components in style. Look for pieces with wire-management holes in the back; holes ringed with smooth brass grommets keep the wood and wires from becoming worn. For low-tech solutions, consider a classic writing desk available in simple Shaker style or with 18th-century-inspired cabriole (curved) legs. A secretary desk, another classic with no relation to the administrative job, features a slender profile, lower drawers, and a drop-down work surface that can stash messy projects fast. Add a hutch on top, either with open shelves or glass-front cabinet doors, for extra display and storage.

The easiest desk solution may be a sturdy, generously sized tabletop secured atop a pair of low two-drawer file cabinets. Extra file cabinets in wood or colorful contemporary

Modular furniture is a logical extension of today's component-style approach. When it comes to study time, your youngster may appreciate the hypermodern look of metals, lunar laminates, and a few special touches like the translucent green drawer pulls shown on this unit. Retailer: Gautier USA, Inc.

metal can also help your student store paperwork in style. For older kids, shop the office furniture sources as well as conventional furniture stores. Office specialty dealers offer a wealth of pieces that will work as hard as your student and last as long as you need them to.

Repetitive stress injuries can have their start in childhood, so whatever arrangement you come up with, don't try to make do with a laptop on a conventional-height work surface for more than an hour at a time. Extended computer work requires a lower work surface, an ergonomic wrist rest, and an office chair with a supportive back and adjustable height. Whether you've got a bookworm or a wiggly worm, it will be easier for your student to concentrate with furniture that makes the grade.

PUT A LITTLE LIGHT ON THE SUBJECT

Even youngsters can suffer eyestrain from inadequate lighting, so don't make do with just a ceiling fixture. Use that to cast ambient general lighting around the room, and supplement with carefully planned task lighting near the bedside and desk. If you do allow electronic screens in the bedroom, position lights so they don't shine on the screen, causing glare, and don't let kids watch TV or use the computer in an otherwise dark room. Situate a shaded 60-watt light along the same plane as the screen to soften harsh contrasts. Don't use halogen lamps in children's rooms; they're very bright but also dangerously hot.

WALL TREATMENTS

Paint is the cheapest decorating tool available, and, once you've moved or covered the furniture and prepped the walls, it's also the easiest and quickest. You can give plain walls

PAINTING BASICS

Like other home improvement techniques discussed in this book, painting is a simple, effective, and affordable way to refresh a room. You don't have to be an expert to achieve a professional finish, but it's best if you follow their advice: Taking time to prepare correctly for the job will help make the actual painting process smooth, flawless, and trouble-free.

What You'll Need

CAULK
SANDPAPER
WOOD-FILLING OR DRYWALL COMPOUND
CLEAN, DAMP CLOTHS
PLASTIC SHEETING
MASKING TAPE
2-INCH-WIDE BLUE PAINTER'S TAPE
PLASTIC KNIFE
PAINTBRUSHES: FLAT, ANGULAR, TRIM
PAINT (1 GALLON FOR EVERY 350 SQUARE FEET)
SMALL PLASTIC PAINT TRAY
PAINT ROLLER AND ROLLER COVER

1. The easiest room to paint is an empty one. If possible, move everything out of the room, including window treatments, and remove hardware such as outlets and switch plates.

2. Repair wall surfaces as needed by filling holes with caulk and smoothing any rough spots with sandpaper. Patch holes with wood-filling or drywall compound; let dry.

3. Wipe surfaces clean with damp cloth. Tape plastic sheeting to floor to protect from spatters, drips, and spills.

4. Use blue painter's tape to cover trims such as window frames and baseboards. Run the blade of a plastic knife over edges of the tape to set edge and prevent paint from leaking underneath.

5. Use a flat brush for painting woodwork, cabinets, and rough-textured surfaces. This brush is also used to cut in, or paint around, the corners, the edges of walls, and the ceiling; a brush spreads paint efficiently and gives you more control than a roller. Cutting in also makes it easier to roll paint onto a wall, since you only have to roll large, flat areas instead of worrying about hard-to-reach places. Use an angular sash brush to paint window sashes; use a trim brush or flat brush for cutting in. When painting with a brush, pour a small amount of paint, about ½ inch, into a small plastic paint tray. Load brush by dipping bristles about ⅓ of the way down into paint. Lightly pat against inside of tray to remove excess. To paint, use long even strokes, always painting from bottom of wall up. Apply enough pressure to flex bristles and distribute paint. Always keep a wet edge on the surface you're painting so paint will dry evenly.

6. Rollers spread paint quickly and easily. This makes them the preferred tool for painting large, flat spaces. However, rollers use more paint and are not as effective as brushes at covering irregular surfaces. To load a paint roller, fill tray with about ½ inch of paint, and dip roller into paint. Lift and run roller over tray ridges or a screen to work paint into nap. The roller should be full but not dripping. Work in small sections, loading roller as needed and rolling up and down until entire surface is covered. As with a brush, it is important to keep a wet edge when rolling paint.

more interest with all kinds of surface treatments, including ragging, stippling, sponge painting, stenciling, and more (see page 59). Painted treatments are easy to keep looking new, provided you use eggshell, semigloss, gloss, or glaze finishes. Just as important, they are easy to change when your child's tastes evolve.

Sponging is one specialty treatment that's easy enough for a grade-schooler to help with under adult direction. Sten-ciling can be a bit tricky, but even a child can work with simple rubber stamps to create a stencillike effect. Whatever treatment you select, be sure to experiment with it on sample boards ahead of time to be sure you like the combination of colors and the overall effect.

Trompe l'oeil (fool the eye) mural painting can open up vistas or bring a fairy tale to life, but, unlike most other faux finishes, it does require real artistic talent. This painting

Painting Ceilings

Always paint ceilings first. Use a trim brush to paint around the edges of the ceiling. Immediately continue by rolling the remainder of the ceiling with a 9-inch-wide roller. For convenience, attach an extension to roller handle so you can paint from the floor.

Painting Walls, Windows, and Doors

After ceiling dries, use a flat brush and a 9-inch-wide roller to paint walls. Cut in walls at ceiling line, corners, and baseboards, and roll remaining portion of wall with paint, always keeping a wet edge.

For windows, try to start painting early in the day so windows will be dry enough to close at night. Remove hardware, then paint woodwork with an angular sash brush.

For doors, remove hardware and, if possible, remove door. Lay flat, and paint with a flat brush.

Painting Trim

Paint standard-width moldings with a trim brush, narrow moldings with a sash brush, and wide moldings with a flat brush. Use a paint shield to pull carpet nap away from baseboards or to protect ceiling and corners. Paint top edge of molding first. The paint should cover any caulk.

Professional Painting Tips

- To keep paint from drying out while you take a break, place the paint roller in the tray and slide the entire tray into a plastic garbage bag; seal. Slide brushes into plastic bags and seal.
- Always follow the grain when painting. Paint horizontally with horizontal sections and vertically with vertical sections.

- Do not paint with a brush that is still wet from cleaning.
- Complete a paint job within 2 weeks. This contributes to adhesion between coats.
- If bristles come off the brush, remove them from the painted surface with tweezers or by touching them with your wet brush—they should cling to it. Then wipe the brush with a clean cloth to remove stray bristles.
- Use painter's tape to prevent paint from bleeding under the tape edge. This tape has a unique microbarrier edge that prevents such seepage, and it won't leave a sticky residue or remove the under-surface when pulled up.
- Use a stenciling brush to work paint into deeply carved wood-work.
- Your painting equipment will last longer if you clean up and properly care for brushes and other tools.
- Clean brushes by swishing in a mixture of warm water and clothes softener. The softener helps paint slide off the brush bristles.
- Store paint in airtight containers. Turn paint can upside down and set on a shelf so the pigments settle at the "bottom." When you use the paint again, turn the can right side up and stir.
- Most paint products are considered hazardous and, as such, should be properly disposed of at an authorized household hazardous waste disposal site. Never pour paint down the drain, onto the ground, or into the trash.
- Wipe empty cans out with newspaper and discard both. Hang solvent-soaked rags outdoors to dry, then launder them. Never store solvent-soaked materials indoors as they can release harmful fumes and catch fire.

Just about any little girl would love a pink ruffled bedroom, but it's the trompe l'oeil garden mural that makes the space special. Even more fun, there's a delicately drawn hilltop castle at the head of the crib. Designer: Betty J. Weir, A Design Shoppe. Artist: Sandy Phelan.

technique is painstaking work, so you may be tempted to keep it even after your child's appreciation has waned. If you really love the idea of trompe l'oeil, keep in mind that a generic nature setting will have a longer life than one depicting the three bears. Murals available on wallcovering rolls are easier to achieve than trompe l'oeil, but they, too, may outstay their welcome as children grow, so be sure to buy a strippable version.

Wallcoverings may be a smart solution to damaged walls you don't want to fix. Stylish themes and color schemes are available these days in easy-care versions that quiet qualms about using them in kids' rooms. You'll want "strippable" products, of course; anyone who's ever scraped vintage paper knows what a labor-intensive chore that can be. For most kids' rooms (family rooms, baths, and kitchens, too), choose washable wallcovering. For younger or very rambunctious kids, you will want wallcovering labeled "scrubbable." Wallcoverings are more work and costlier than paint, however, so be sure your youngster is pleased before you make a purchase.

DECORATIVE FINISHES

A child's room is the perfect place to let one's personality shine through. An effective way to do this is with decorative finishes. Once you've settled on a design, use the following finishes on ordinary furniture—even walls and doors—to add oomph to any decor.

Brush Pattern

With a dry paintbrush, dab texture paint onto the wall. Use a quick, short, patting motion, varying the direction of the brush to create ridges and patterns.

Colorwashing

To colorwash, apply a thin, transparent coat of waterbase paint to surface. Use broad, arcing strokes to spread paint. When dry, add additional layers until color achieves an intense depth with subtle variations in tone.

Crackling

When achieved with traditional wood stain colors, crackling gives furniture an aged effect. Use pastels or bright primary paint colors, however, and the effect is totally contemporary.

Most paint stores sell kits with everything you need for a crackle finish. If you want to work with colors you have at home, basecoat surface with paint, and let dry. Using a fitch or small paintbrush, apply a coat of oilbase crackling varnish over entire surface. When varnish is almost dry but still tacky to the touch, apply another coat of the varnish. The crackling effect will appear as the varnish dries. If desired, use a hair dryer to speed up the process. When all coats of varnish are dry, rub a tinted glaze or coat of paint onto surface with a soft, clean rag. The glaze or paint will lodge into the cracks and accentuate the crackling effect.

Decoupage

Like stenciling, decoupage is an easy way to add interesting motifs to ordinary furniture. Anything from wallpaper to photographs to magazines can be used for decoupaging, and you can apply 1 specific image or overlap images to cover the entire surface of the furniture.

Basecoat piece of furniture or other surface; let dry. For specific designs, cut out images to be used. For an overall finish, trim papers as desired. Apply decoupage medium or a mixture of 1 part white glue and 1 part water to back of image. Press onto furniture. Brush mixture over top of image to seal. Continue adding desired images or papers, overlapping as needed. Always brush medium over top of image to seal. Let dry. When design is complete, apply a coat of nonyellowing waterbase varnish to entire surface.

Dragging

When used with some paint colors, such as pink or green, dragging can simulate wood grain. To drag a surface, basecoat it, and let dry. Pour a small amount of paint into tray. Dip a dry, wide, stiff brush into paint. Dab onto paper to remove excess, then brush in 1 continuous stroke over surface. Continue adding strokes to entire surface, using even pressure and replenishing paint as necessary for even finish.

Ragging

Ragging also creates color contrast and texture, but the result is less consistent than sponging. To achieve the look, apply a basecoat (usually the lighter paint color) to surface; let dry. Dip a lint-free rag, scrunched-up paper sack, or plastic bag into a contrasting emulsion paint. Dab to remove excess, then press randomly over surface. Use light, even pressure, and replenish paint as necessary for even finish. For different effects, vary the amount of paint on the rag, the amount of pressure applied, and the direction in which you hold your hand. Change rag as it becomes saturated with paint.

Sponging

Quick and easy to apply, sponging is one of the most popular types of finishes. Expect an even finish, or, if you choose 2 or 3 contrasting colors, you'll get a speckled pattern. To sponge a surface, basecoat wall or furniture with lightest paint color; let dry. Dip a damp natural sponge into paint, dab on paper to remove excess, and lightly press over surface. Use even pressure and replenish paint as necessary for an even finish. Change sponge as it becomes saturated with paint.

Stippling

Stippling is a simple way to add texture to a flat surface. To stipple, apply a basecoat to wall or furniture. Let dry. Pour a small amount of paint into paint tray. Use a 1¼-inch-nap roller cover or a texture roller cover. Roll it through paint in smooth strokes similar to those used to lay off paint. To produce an even, overall pattern like that of a sprayed textured ceiling, work slowly to avoid overlapping, and apply consistent pressure from 1 side to the other. Vary the pressure and direction of your strokes to make a random pattern.

Swirl Pattern

Use a whisk broom or wallpaper brush to sweep semicircular loops across the surface. Overlap the loops as you go.

Trowel Pattern

Apply textured paint to surface, and let it become almost dry. Then trowel over the paint to knock off the peaks and partially smooth out the texture.

Whimsically buggy wallpaper gets an extra wacky touch from a supersize mural that includes a growth chart on one side. Since kids' tastes change, you'll want to choose a wallcovering that's scrubbable today and strippable tomorrow. Manufacturer: Blonder Wallcoverings.

If you're not sure about using wallcovering throughout your child's room, use wallpaper borders as an easy and colorful alternative. Choose your border first, however, and then find a paint that matches one of the dominant colors in the border. You'll find it infinitely easier than trying to find a border that matches a paint choice. (This advice also applies to selecting wallcoverings before you select your trim paint, broadloom carpeting, etc.)

For real textural interest, you may want to embellish the room with beadboard paneling below the chair-rail level. Beadboard is especially appealing in a cottage- or cabin-inspired room. Wood trim millwork available at home centers can also be used to add depth and charm; lightweight, paintable resin versions are available, too.

Don't overlook the ceiling as another major surface to decorate. While too much detail or intense colors will overwhelm the typical room, children will delight in a cloud-filled blue sky overhead and find nighttime comfort in stick-on glow-in-the-dark stars.

WALLPAPERING BASICS

Since its creation, wallpaper has been an invaluable way to add patterns, architectural features, and details to an otherwise ordinary room. Modern children's rooms are no exception. Indeed, with the variety of styles and colors on the market, wallpapering is one of the easiest ways to create a specific decorating scheme in a room. A bonus for children's rooms: Wallpaper is durable and can be quickly cleaned, making it easy to remove smudgy hand prints and impromptu drawings!

What You'll Need

PREPASTED WALLPAPER
PENCIL
PLUMBLINE AND CHALK
RULER
WATER
WALLPAPER BRUSH
BROAD KNIFE
UTILITY KNIFE

1. Remove outlet covers, switch plates, and other protrusions from the walls.

2. Next, identify the room's focal point. This is usually directly across from the door or in the center of the wall you see upon entering the bedroom.

3. Center roll of wallpaper over focal point, and mark wall on both sides of the wallpaper to determine placement. Snap a plumb line where the right edge of the wallpaper will be placed.

4. From the plumb line and working from both sides of the piece marked at the focal point, measure and mark wallpaper placement on both sides of each strip around to the dead corner, which is the most inconspicuous corner in the room. This corner usually falls near the door.

5. Measure and cut several sheets of wallpaper. Roll each sheet with the pattern on the outside. This will help take the twist out of the paper.

6. Place a rolled sheet of wallpaper into lukewarm water, and let it soak according to manufacturer's instructions.

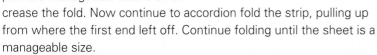

7. Remove wallpaper from water and "book" the strip. To do this, fold 1 end of the strip toward the middle of the sheet, pasted sides together, so that the folded part is a manageable size. Do not crease the fold. Now continue to accordion fold the strip, pulling up from where the first end left off. Continue folding until the sheet is a manageable size.

8. Working from the top of the wall and centered over the marked focal point, unfold the top portion of the booked wallpaper. Align the right edge of the sheet with the plumb line, and press the paper to the wall, leaving a 2-inch margin of paper at the top and positioning the key element in the wallpaper design as desired.

9. Smooth the sheet with a wallpaper brush, and crease the 2-inch margin at the top of the wall so that the margin flaps over onto the ceiling. Continue to position the remaining portion of the wallpaper sheet. Crease at the bottom of the wall so that the 2-inch margin overlaps the baseboard.

10. Using a utility knife, trim paper at the top and bottom of the wall. For a smooth cut, use the broad knife as a guide and avoid lifting the knife blade as you cut.

11. After hanging several sheets, wash the walls and baseboards with a clean, wet cloth to remove any wallpaper paste.

Wallpapering Around Obstacles
Make sure electricity is turned off. Wallpaper over holes in the wall left by outlets and light switches, then cut along the sides of the outlet or light switch. Lift the paper slightly, and trim along the top and bottom portion of the outlet or light switch box.

Covering Switch and Outlet Plates
Match wallpaper to the design on the wall around the opening, then cut a piece for the outlet or switch plate, 1 inch larger on all sides. Use adhesive spray on the outside of the plate and cover with the wallpaper, wrapping sides around to the back. Cut an X in the center of outlet and switch holes to all 4 corners, then fold wallpaper to underside of plate.

Wallpapering Tips
- Always remove existing wallpaper before hanging new wallpaper. Rent a steamer or buy a chemical peeler, or hire a professional.
- Start in a basic room with flat, open areas and few doors and windows or in a room where a mistake won't be apparent.
- Two installers are better than one. Successful installation relies on an assembly-line method, with 1 person cutting and prepping the paper and the other person hanging the paper. Working together in this method contributes to efficiency and success.
- To prevent mold and fungus from growing underneath the wallpaper, choose a wallpaper paste that contains fungicides.
- Use yellow chalk to snap plumb lines. Blue chalk can bleed through the wallpaper.
- Wrap wallpaper around outside corners to prevent having an edge that can tear or lift at the corner. Cut wallpaper along inside corners to avoid puckering.
- Never overlap wallpaper.
- Most bubbles disappear as the wallpaper dries. For any remaining bubbles, make a V-cut in the center of the bubble. Lift the flap and moisten, then smooth in place.
- A stripe or random-match pattern is the easiest pattern for beginners to hang. The next choice is a straight-across match, where half the pattern is at the edge of 1 sheet and the other half is directly across from it on the next sheet.

STENCILING

Incorporate flora, fauna—even cartoon characters—into a decor by stenciling designs onto furniture and walls. Stencils were created as an alternative to more expensive wallpaper, but their popularity has grown so that today stenciling is often a preferred technique.

Prep Time

Use either oilbase or waterbase paint, but either should be a creamy consistency—not so thick as to clog the brush but not thin enough to run behind the stencil. Matte and satin finishes look best. Also consider specialty stencil crayons that work much like paints.

Stencil brushes have short, stiff bristles and come in a variety of sizes. You will need several brushes, one for each color used. This keeps colors from becoming muddy and also speeds things up because you won't have to clean your brush between colors. Match the size of the brush to the size of the area to be painted: The brush should be about half the size of the area to be painted. If the whole stencil will be 1 color, a bigger brush is fine because it will allow you to work more quickly. You may want to experiment with other applicators, such as sponges or spray paint, to get different looks.

Applying Paint

There are 2 basic techniques you can use with a stencil brush. Each gives a slightly different look, and you might find one easier to do than the others.

Stippling—Hold brush perpendicular to surface, and tap up and down with brush to apply color. The effect is that of lots of little dots created by the bristles. With stippling, the stencil is less likely to move around so you're less likely to get paint under the edges.

Swirling—This technique is generally used with stencil crèmes, not acrylic paints. To create a smooth finish, hold brush perpendicular to surface, letting it rest just on the surface. Swirl brush in small circles to color in area. Don't push paint under edges of stencil. With swirling, there will be some buildup of paint around the edges.

Adding Shading

When working with just 1 color, start on outside edges of opening and work toward center. This creates a shadowed edge and highlighted center, adding depth without additional colors. Darken the color by applying more pressure to brush, not more paint.

When using more than 1 color, start with the lightest color first to fill in space and create highlight. Then use darker color worked from outside edge into center. You can also dry-brush a darker color to create a shadow effect on the very edges.

Let's Paint!

While stenciling is not difficult, it does require knowledge of a few basic techniques. Take the time to practice before painting on the real surface. This is also the time to test the colors you've chosen and to experiment with shading. Once you're confident in your growing skills, move on to your project.

What You'll Need

STENCIL DESIGN
CHALK
PLUMB LINE OR YARDSTICK
MASKING TAPE OR PAINTER'S TAPE
STENCIL PAINTS
STENCIL BRUSH OR SMALL SPONGE
CLEAN, DAMP CLOTH

1. Mark position of stencil design on wall with chalk. Use plumb line or yardstick to make sure stencil is level and centered as desired.

2. Using stencil as a template, make registration marks by positioning stencil on wall and marking each corner placement with chalk.

3. To apply more than 1 color, use masking or painter's tape to cover all the areas you don't want to paint first.

4. Use masking tape to secure stencil to surface. Align corners with registration marks.

5. Using as little paint as possible, dip stencil brush or sponge into paint, and stipple or swirl paint onto surface, working from middle of stencil to the outside. Be careful not to use too much paint, as it may seep underneath stencil.

6. When paint is dry, remove stencil and wipe away excess paint from stencil pattern with a clean, damp cloth. Continue by repositioning and stenciling designs in same color before stenciling additional colors of the design.

Making Your Own Stencils

Sometimes you just can't find the stencil you want. Now what? Almost any kind of clear plastic will make a good stencil because it won't absorb paint and you can see through it to trace a design. Another option, though not as durable as plastic, is cardstock and poster board. Trace design on plastic or cardstock, then cut it out with a sharp craft knife. Try to cut in 1 continuous line; the piece should just fall out when you're done. Test out your stencil to see how closely it creates the image you want. When you're satisfied, start stenciling!

Whatever wall treatment you are contemplating, if your house is old, be careful of leadbase paint, especially in a child's room. Painting over leadbase paint is usually considered safer than scraping it off, but be sure to consult your local public health office for specific recommendations for your situation.

FLOORING

Stain-resistant low-pile broadloom carpeting is great for kids' rooms and family rooms. It's warm, cushions the inevitable bumps, and helps muffle noise. Hard-surface flooring (wood, ceramic tile, vinyl tile, etc.) is a sensible alternative that's easy to keep clean and offers a great surface for racing mini cars and rolling out modeling clay. You may want to combine both in one room to create two separate zones for different activities. A more common alternative is to warm up a wood or tile floor with an area rug or two, but be sure to use nonskid pads beneath rugs—even large ones. Avoid scratchy, hard-to-clean sisal in favor of nylon, olefin, wool, or cotton. You'll want to have rugs and carpeting cleaned annually for health's sake, but to hide soil and stains between cleanings, choose midtone shades rather than very light or very dark ones, or pick multicolor patterned designs. Self-stick carpet squares are easy to install and very practical; buy enough initially so you can replace any squares that become damaged.

Wood is the most versatile choice for whole-house use, but vinyl, cork, or even rubber tiles also take some of the

Dramatic area rugs, from colorful wool to soft faux fur, add lively pattern and texture to a room inspired by a playful take on the Old West. Rug designs to fit almost any motif are available; they can reinforce your decorating theme as they boost the coziness quotient.

PAINTING AND REFINISHING WOOD FLOORS

While carpet certainly feels nice underfoot, wood floors are much more practical in a child's room. Broken crayons, glitter sprinkles, spilled paints—pretty much everything is easier to clean off of a wood floor.

Like most other surfaces, wood floors must first be properly cleaned and repaired for a successful finish. The easiest way to do this is to hire a professional refinisher. If you decide to take on the project yourself, it is essential that you rent an industrial floor sander.

Prep Time

To begin, remove everything from the room, and open windows to keep air circulating. Using a rough grade of sandpaper on the industrial floor sander, begin sanding the floor in a diagonal direction. Work back and forth, covering as much of the room as possible. When the entire floor has been covered, switch to a finer grade of sandpaper and work up and down the boards, following the wood grain. Finish around the edges of the room with a belt sander, again following the grain if possible. Vacuum the room, and wipe down the floors and walls with a clean, damp rag to remove dust.

Finishes

There are several ways to finish a wood floor. The most common way is to **stain** the wood. This works well if the floor is not dam-aged, allowing the wood grain to shine through. Working from 1 side of the room to the other, apply wood stain in the desired color to the floor with a cloth. Follow manufacturer's instructions, keeping amount of stain even as you work across the room.

For a light finish, consider **bleaching** the boards. Follow manufacturer's instructions for best results. Using a commercial 2-part bleach (available at home supply stores), apply the first part of the bleach to the entire floor. This usually darkens the wood slightly. Apply the second part of the bleach. To neutralize the bleach, wash it off after 2 coats. Lightly sand floor with industrial floor sander to even out raised grains of wood.

For damaged floors or to add color to a room, **paint** the floors just as you would a wall. Choose oilbase paints for a hard film; this type of paint also covers damaged surfaces well. Latex paint has a resilient finish and allows the surface to breathe. It works well in damp climates.

Sealing

The final step in refinishing or painting a wood floor is to seal the finish. Nonyellowing polyurethane is probably the easiest sealer to work with, and it is available in both oilbase and waterbase finishes. Following manufacturer's instructions, apply the first coat, and let dry completely. Follow with 2 more coats for a hard, durable finish. If needed, sand between coats, wiping away dust with a clean, damp cloth.

"hard" out of hard-surface flooring. Ceramic, porcelain, and natural stone tiles are beautiful but are also very hard, and tumbles are a part of life for kids. If you use one of these, you'll want to be sure to add a generously sized area rug to play areas and around the bed.

WINDOW TREATMENTS

A child's room is no place for swooping draperies or dangling cords, but you do want to provide for light control so children can nap during the day and have privacy at night. Wood shutters are charming and substantial; those that cover only the bottom half of the window protect privacy but let in light, so you'll want to add roller shades or Roman shades on top.

Gathered Roman shades, handsome even in simple canvas, look wonderful in a circus stripe. Pleated shades come in a variety of tints and patterns; bottom-mount versions can be pulled up from the sill to let in light but protect privacy.

Bamboo roller shades are available in colors as well as natural and dramatic tortoiseshell (gold and dark brown) hues, but even the simplest white cloth or vinyl roller shades can be ornamented with a variety of decorative treatments. A roller shade on top with simple café-length curtains below is perhaps the easiest and most economical solution; cotton-poly blend curtains are widely available in a great range of colors and patterns and are very easy to care for.

ACCESSORIES

Adorable accessories of every kind imaginable are widely available for children's rooms. If you're starting from scratch, remember what may look like cozy clutter in a magazine picture can become total chaos when you add the multitudes of stuffed animals, blocks, and dolls that proliferate throughout real kids' rooms. Try to keep it simple, and let your kids (and doting relatives) fill in the gaps.

Bypassing the bulk of impulse items out there doesn't mean skipping delightful decorating opportunities. While kids may enjoy finding fun accessories and choosing fabrics and paint colors, most aren't really interested in decorating for its own sake. So instead of accumulating dust catchers, look for clothing hooks, mirrors, mouse pads, pillows, pencil cups, and scores of other practical items to fit your color scheme or fantasy theme. If your child has a hobby or passion, encourage family members to give gifts that relate.

When you're on vacation, try to steer older kids clear of the usual souvenirs in favor of picture frames and other accessories they will enjoy longer. One exception may be if your child has a collection. He or she will already be exercising some self-editing by looking for collectibles rather than impulse items. In this case, help show off a precious collection with a display case (for older kids) or simple shelving mounted around the perimeter of the room. If the collectibles are also playthings, display them where your child can easily reach them—and put them back.

MEASURING WINDOWS FOR BLINDS AND CURTAINS

When fitting a window with blinds or curtains, it's critical to get the correct measurements. So, before purchasing any window treatments, make a copy of the window shown here, measure your window accordingly, then write down the measurements along the corresponding arrows. Take this handy chart with you when shopping for curtains and blinds or when meeting with a decorator or seamstress.

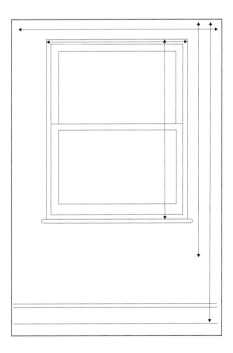

Except for privacy shades, kids' rooms can do without heavy window treatments. You can still soften the look and enhance the room's scheme with a crisp valance using motifs, fabrics, and colors from the rest of the room. Designer: Angela Rowe, INTERIORS by Decorating Den.

Decorating Ideas

You'll want to plan some elements of your child's room to last for years, but you'll also want the room to please and nurture your child at each stage of development. Babies, toddlers, grade-schoolers, preteens, and teens each have wants and needs a thoughtfully designed room can help fulfill. In addition to needs specific to age, a child's gender and individual tastes will also influence your choices. Use this portfolio of appealing ideas to jump-start your creative decision-making, and involve your child as much as possible. Here's a case where one picture may reveal just what your youngster had in mind.

A color scheme of turquoise and lime is one that would add pep to any youngster's step! Plenty of space to stash books and magazines, photos, and other stuff is a must—especially as she gets older. Manufacturer: Brewster Wallcovering Co.

Baby Nurseries

From the moment you bring your precious infant home, his or her (or their!) room will become a special place for you and your child. Even if you keep your baby in your bedroom at night for the first few settling-in months, you'll probably use the baby's room for changing diapers and other everyday tasks. The sooner you and your child feel comfortable in the nursery, the better. (Yes, you need to feel at home in the baby's room, too, as you'll be spending a lot of hours there!)

In addition to a crib that meets modern safety standards, you'll want a comfortable easy chair or cushioned rocking chair to coddle you while you cuddle your little one. If you are nursing or just want a little extra support for your back, be sure to include a footstool that's a comfortable height for you. While you're thinking of major furniture pieces, a twin bed or daybed is a good idea for those inevitable long nights when you're up and down with a sick or fretful little one. (Besides, your child will grow into that twin bed almost before you know it!)

You may think that any sturdy chest, dresser, or table can be used as a changing table, but the safest solution is a conventional changing table with a built-in low rail around the perimeter of the changing pad. (The rail should be at least a few inches higher than the pad to help keep baby from rolling off.) If you use a unit that doesn't have a rail, be sure to install a securely anchored safety strap around baby's middle and use it *every* time. Why all the fuss about safety? Because, as any experienced parent can tell you, babies beyond the newborn stage seem able to move farther and faster than you'd think possible! Also look for a changing table with one or two open lower shelves that let you grab diapering supplies with one hand—and fast. If you use a closed storage unit, you'll want to pick one that you can open with one hand (most wide drawers require even pressure on two pulls) or plan to take out whatever you need before starting the process.

Once you've got the crib, comfy chair, changing table, and optional extra bed in place, the rest is child's play. If your family includes older children who share baby's room, their needs will obviously dictate a lot of the furnishings and accessories.

or fairy-tale images and your budget can accommodate them, why not indulge? You (and other adults and older kids in the family) can enjoy them now, knowing your child will be able to appreciate them when he or she reaches preschool age. Do remember that children as old as seven have trouble distinguishing what's real from what's imaginary, so make sure the images you provide aren't scary ones. Especially in a bedroom, you'll want the mood to be comforting not disturbing.

Just about any color scheme can work, but it's usually best to keep colors on the clear, light side. Little ones don't usually like sophisticated gray tones, and dark shades can make the typical small bedroom feel and look even smaller. In these pages, you'll see how light, cheerful tints such as mint green, yellow, and timeless white, combined with a variety of special accents, can look fresh and delightfully personal. What a nice way to start out life!

If the room is for the baby only, you may be tempted to go for broke with decorative treatments. There's no harm in doing this as long as you avoid items with small parts or cords, but you don't have to spend a fortune on special effects. Babies can't really see details or pick out the nuances of color until they're six months old or so. Until then, bold patterns in black and white serve much better to stimulate their eyes and brains.

If your taste tends toward the lively and modern, a baby's room in black and white with red accents may be just the ticket. If not, however, you can provide short-term toys and board books that stimulate baby just as well and decorate in a way that better suits your style.

Elaborate trompe l'oeil treatments that parade favorite characters across the walls are quite popular, as you'll see in the following pages. Do keep in mind, however, that babies and even toddlers can't appreciate the finer points of such artwork just yet. If you have your heart set on nursery rhyme

Pattern Play

Intricate patterns galore create a visual feast in this extraordinary room inspired by treasures of the Far East. This exciting space boasts a unique focal point: A lacquered, gilded armoire covered in elaborate scenes is a delight for the eyes. Boldly overscaled for a conventional-size children's bedroom, the antique reproduction armoire delivers big drama that won't be outgrown. In keeping with the Asian-inspired mood, black lacquered children's furniture is sculpturally handsome. To keep the look from being too formal or severe, a lovely aqua tint covers the walls and floor. Asian-inspired fabrics with bright clear colors on white backgrounds add a fresh lighthearted air. Long after the crib is gone, this room's dramatic heirloom look will still be going strong.

Black furniture, made of lacquered or ebonized wood, has a long tradition that's international and very dramatic. Against beautifully colored walls, the effect is exciting and quite contemporary. Commode: Grange. Lamp: Forrest Jones.

The spectacular reproduction armoire elevates this child's room to heirloom status. A simple rod hung at ceiling-trim level shows off charming draperies and makes the most of a big graceful window. The coordinating changing table can be used as a dresser when diaper changing duties are done (see page 39 for information on safe changing tables). Designer: Karen Graham Interiors. Armoire: IMG. Crib and dresser/changing table: Vermont Precision.

Patterns inspired by Asian art find a special new home in a treasured baby's room. The pristine white backgrounds and bright jewel tones create a look that's lively yet precise. (Be sure to remove pillow before putting baby to bed.) Fabric: Schumacher.

71

Tender Tints

There's no doubt that the little one who occupies this room is treasured. Located on the ground floor, the room's garden views are echoed in the delicate green-and-white color scheme within. If you don't know whether you're having a girl or a boy (or want to bypass the usual pink or blue view), consider a scheme of gentle mint green sparked with yellow and soothed with white. It's versatile, harmonious, and pleasant to be in. The special feeling is enhanced by subtle touches, especially walls covered in shirred white fabric. A mix of romantically shaped furniture pieces, all painted white, creates a sweet nostalgic look. Above, a pale blue sky textured with clouds is one more quietly magical effect.

A storage cabinet stashes diapers and supplies out of sight, but, because it's white wicker, the piece is visually light and unobtrusive. A soft pad with a wipe-clean cover turns it into a pretty changing table (see page 39 for information on safe changing tables).

A pretty armoire gains even more eye appeal with storybook illustrations painted on each panel in sweet pastels. Victorian-inspired wicker furniture is pretty, and its rounded edges make things safer. (Floor plants are fine for infant rooms, but remove them when baby starts crawling.)

In the Pink

A graceful roll-arm sofa serves several purposes in this young girl's room and looks charming, too, thanks to its mix of fresh fabrics. A low cottage-style bench can stand in as a stool for little climbers and as a coffee table for adult visitors.

This little girl's room already has the air of a delightful studio apartment. When she outgrows the crib, the rest of the room will be one she can enjoy and be proud of. While it's as feminine as her heart might desire, the room is also versatile and chic. Against a garden scheme of pink, green, and white, cottage-style pieces, including an old-fashioned glider, provide vintage charm. The attractive sofa and window treatment, however, are suitable for any room. The couch makes things more comfortable for parents during late-night vigils with a sick little one, and it's fun for daytime giggles and cuddles, too. When she's a bit older, the sofa will make a nice berth for a sleepover guest.

A vintage quilt with its interesting hues helps take a pink-and-white room beyond the predictable. A quilt is the perfect artwork for a baby's room; it's as colorful as a painting but safer for curious little ones.

Subtle tints of pink fill this room, but the effect isn't overly sweet thanks to the use of mostly tailored checked prints. Distressed white furniture has a relaxed look; the end table's lower shelf is a great place to stash stuffed animals and books.

An apple green crib ensemble featuring animals from Noah's ark inspired this fresh decorating scheme for a little boy's room. A custom rug bordered with lions, elephants, and more underscores the timelessly appealing theme. Designer: Karen Cashman, Perspectives.

Sunshine yellow makes a cheerful background for a little boy's room that celebrates planes, trains, and automobiles. A colorful crib ensemble brings out lively accent hues throughout the room. Designer: Pamela DiCapo. Retailer: Lauren Alexandra.

Color Play

Two of the most popular themes for little boys' rooms are animals and vehicles. These two spaces make charming use of such tried-and-true concepts with a wealth of designer details and enticing color schemes. In one room, a Noah's ark theme starts with fresh apple green and medium blue then punches it up with shots of red and other warm hues. In the other, sunny yellow stripes and checks make a cheerful background for planes, cars, and other vehicles in green and red. A multicolor crib ensemble and deftly upholstered mini wing chairs add even more charm. Rambunctious or studious, a little boy's imagination can still be sparked by a clever, kid-friendly design. Start with a motif you think he'll love, and take off from there!

Checkerboard Table

What You'll Need
Wooden table, at least 20 inches square
Sandpaper
Damp cloth
Paintbrushes
Acrylic paints: white, blue, red, and yellow
Clean, dry cloth
Pencil
Ruler
Painter's tape
Clear-drying matte acrylic varnish

1. Sand top and edges of table smooth. Wipe clean with damp cloth.

2. Using medium-size paintbrush, paint table white. For aged effect, use clean, dry cloth to gently rub paint away from edges of tabletop and legs. To add color to sides, paint only sides yellow (not legs). When dry, randomly draw 1-inch-diameter circles on yellow sides with red paint.

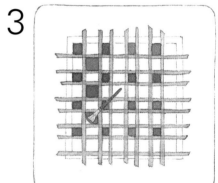

3. Draw a 12-inch square in center of table, 4 inches from each edge. Mark square into 8 rows and columns, using 1½-inch squares to form a checkerboard pattern. Draw 1-inch-wide line around checkerboard for border. Place painter's tape on outside of every other square on 1st, 3rd, 5th, and 7th rows; paint blue. Let dry, then carefully remove tape. Repeat for remaining even-numbered rows, this time alternating between painted squares on odd-numbered lines. Let dry; remove tape. Finally, position painter's tape along inside and outside lines of border, and paint red.

4. When checkerboard is complete, paint 2 coats of clear-drying matte acrylic varnish over entire table.

The ruffle-canopied crib is the room's focal point now, but, in a few years, the nearby daybed will take center stage. (An extra bed makes sense in baby's room anyway for those late-night feedings and when you're on 24-hour nurse duty.) The pretty changing table can stash a lot, now and later.

Sweetness and Light

A bank of windows floods this baby girl's room with light on sunny days, but, even when it's gloomy out, it's bright inside. Awash in space-expanding, pristine white, the walls and floor are treated to subtle pastel ribbons, all lovingly hand-painted. Pink nosegays are everywhere: Painted ones tint the walls, silk versions decorate the frothy white window valances, and baby rosebud prints cover the crib and changing table. Despite the delicate look, the room includes all the practical necessities: washable cotton fabrics, a comfortable rocking chair with a reading lamp, a good-size toy chest, and a changing table with extra storage shelves. The result is as smart as it is pretty, just like this room's cherished little occupant.

Dolls and collectibles adorn the bank of windows in this spacious room with plenty of space for later floor play. Frills and furbelows set the sentimental mood in a few key areas. An elaborate but lighthearted Victorian wicker rocker works well with a cutwork-shaded floor lamp; the toy chest is dressed up as a dollhouse.

Minty Fresh

Green, the color of growing things, is a perennial favorite in rooms for little ones. Paired with pink and white for girls, it makes a garden statement without half trying. Grouped with blue and white, as it is here, green makes a refreshing preserve for a little boy. Hand-painted stylized waves and bubbly circles, together with playful contemporary furniture, create a simple setting that's sure to please. Just about any pastel tint you like could be used for similar results. Just be sure to use it with analogous, or closely allied, tints for a flowing not choppy effect. In a south- or west-facing room, cool tints of green, blue, and periwinkle (blue-violet) work best; in a space that faces north or east, try warm tints of yellow, peach, and coral or pink.

Twin cribs get distinctive looks with two different crib bumper fabrics. Each piece of furniture is as simple as can be, but the look is wonderfully special thanks to a vision realized in paint. Stylist: Amy Leonard. Manufacturer: The Glidden Company.

A cute little wall shelf with rounded brackets echoes the lighthearted feeling of the room. Look for attractive economical shelves and brackets like these at home improvement stores and unfinished furniture shops.

Dresser drawers in alternating tints and hand-painted wavy stripes and circles create a gently playful look on this changing table (see page 39 for information on safe changing tables).

Forecast: Sunshine

A confident eye for color and a sure hand with fabrics are both apparent in this whimsical room. Avoiding the usual clichés, the space is wonderfully clever as well as pretty and soothing. A cute room might use a faux finish to suggest a blue sky with white clouds; this room goes beyond cute to captivating by adding a trio of flying geese, one of them garbed as Mother Goose. A nicely shaped easy chair and ottoman are always a comfort, but here they reach the realm of art furniture thanks to various cheery fabrics and contrasting piping. Even a simple white lamp shade gets a perky outlook with glued-on pink pompons. The hand-painted golden motif on floor and pillows says it all: This room was born with a sunny disposition.

An already distressed green table and chairs will handle all the tea parties youngsters can dish out. A cloud-strewn blue sky overhead enhances the outdoor picnic feeling.

Skip the droopy machine-made lace and skimpy satin ribbons: Here, retro pompons, primitive-style sun motifs, and a mix of crisp cotton ruffles create a look that's girlish yet contemporary. (For safety reasons, be sure to always remove pillows before putting baby to bed.) A subtle trompe l'oeil ivy twines along the driftwood-finished bed.

Mother Goose and friends spread sheltering wings over the crib in this endearing, imaginative baby's room. The handsome window carries a fairy-tale message with casually opulent swags in sky blue, yellow, and rose. Designer: Pamela DiCapo. Retailer: Lauren Alexandra.

A Warm Welcome

Kids love warm colors, and even a young baby can recognize red. If you've been reluctant to use conventional fire engine red in large doses, consider one of the rich, interesting alternative reds shown here. Coral, cranberry, barn red, and other ruby hues inject a feeling that's both exciting and cozy. The trick to keeping red manageable is balance. If you opt for red walls, keep the ceiling, floor, furniture, and accessories cool and light. White, cream, pale blue, and light green add serenity to offset red's stimulation. If you choose red furniture that covers a smaller area of the room, you can easily use warm tints on the walls and floor. Yellow, pink, peach, or melon gently continues the warming trend.

A glider and ottoman are comfortable for mother as well as baby. This room is ready for a baby girl, but the red, yellow, and green accents would work just as well in a boy's room. Designer: Claudia Adetuyi, Adeeni Associates.

Rich cranberry walls are elegant—and they're pretty good at hiding scuffs and fingerprints, too. To keep the room from looking oppressively dark, bleached wood floors and bright white furniture lighten the mood. Manufacturer: EG Furniture.

Deep barn red delivers all the warmth of scarlet but without the bite. It's perfect for a room inspired by rustic colonial American style. Here, creamy ivory, gold, Federal blue, and natural wood tones carry out the look. Retailer: The Magic Moon.

85

Engaging Enchantment

Amusingly leaded vintage windows inspired this charming nursery in a venerable house. Creating a child-friendly nest while honoring the dramatic architecture was the goal. One window depicting a leaping bunny worked fine for a nursery, but a new idea was needed to keep the other window's imagery of cats and a pumpkin from looking like Halloween. The designer chose a theme of Mother Goose's garden to tie in these and other animals and plants. Eventually, the room included cows jumping over the moon, cabbages, a rocking horse, and the fluffy old storytelling fowl herself. Lots of white and pastel tints are balanced by rich dark wood tones and antique artworks. The effect is a lightened-up Victorian-style nursery that looks historically rich yet delicate and fresh.

Yards of tulle cascade down upon an heirloom-style iron crib that captures the light from whimsically leaded windows. Pumpkins and cabbages, the designer's signature images, appear in a room inspired by Mother Goose's garden. Custom cornice boards and window boxes give the windows even more panache. Designer: Jennifer Norris, Jennifer Norris Interiors.

A hand-painted mural in gentle pastel tints depicts Mother Goose in a shawl and slippers. On the wall, vintage children's book illustrations add nostalgic interest and tie in the deeper shades of the rich wood floor.

An antique pine dresser stores blankets, baby clothes, diapers, and more. Even better, it stays true to the room's vintage look. Simply framed nursery prints are hung casually by ribbons from pegs along the wall.

Little Boy Blue

For a lucky baby boy, this spacious bedroom features a look that's bright, light, charming, and sophisticated—all at the same time. It's also thoughtfully designed for safety and comfort. The secret of this engaging room is the smooth mix of classic and chic elements. The design starts with the tried-and-true scheme of medium blue and white and the traditional patterns of mini checks and shirting stripes, but it doesn't stop there. A delightfully distinctive graphic of circus animals sets the room apart. The graphic creates visual excitement on the crib as well as on the easy chair and draperies. Graceful, simple contemporary furniture adds to the subtle appeal; when the crib is outgrown, the rest of the room will still be a winner.

A big cushy glider and ottoman make a nice alternative to a rocking chair. Whichever you choose, a chair that's comfortable for adults is a must for bedtime stories, low-key play, and lots of cuddling.

A white crib that's shapely but not frilly gets an extra kick from whimsical circus illustrations taken from the charming chair and drapery fabric. These parents have wisely kept artwork high up on the wall, out of reach, and given baby a mobile overhead. Designer: Nursery Lines Ltd.

A simple, gracefully shaped dresser that's wider than most works as a practical changing table for now (see page 39 for information on safe changing tables). A small-scale lamp with a low-wattage bulb makes midnight diaper changing a bit more comfortable for everyone.

Sunny Disposition

Hey, diddle diddle, there's no better way to bring a sunshine mood to a baby's room than with nursery rhymes and a yellow, white, and sky blue color scheme. In this cheery nest under the eves, Humpty Dumpty, the cow jumping over the moon, and other timeless favorites are rendered in masterful trompe l'oeil illustrations. Even without these creations, however, the decorating scheme is one that both girls and boys would love. A merry mix of patterns, all variations on stripes, add visual movement to the space, but the large expanses of pale solid colors keep the overall look soothing. A setting like this is delightful proof that you don't need a big room to make a big splash for your little one.

An elaborate Victorian rocker gets a delightfully fresh look with glossy white paint and a circus-stripe cushion. The yellow-and-white-stripe fabric with tiny detailed figures is cute on its own, but it's the piped blue-and-white-stripe fabric used as trim that gives it a decorator look.

A white chest of drawers and Gothic-style shelf get star treatment with a mix of real and trompe l'oeil toys and accessories. Even the part of the shelf Humpty's sitting on is hand-painted. You could use this technique to bring fairies, butterflies, a favorite animal, or other fanciful motifs into a room.

A hand-painted cow jumping over the moon is a savvy choice on an eave wall where a framed picture wouldn't work. The deep crib skirt is another smart move, offering lots of hidden storage with style.

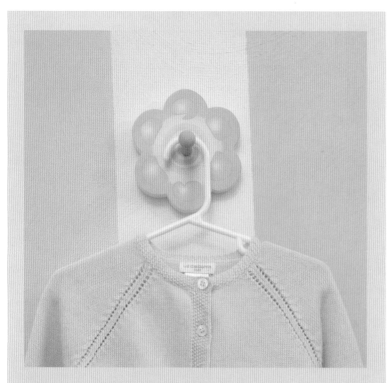

All in Fun

Color is the most emotionally compelling element in any design, so there's no quicker way to create a happy mood than to use cheerful hues like the ones shown here. Sounds simple, but simplicity may be exactly what you want in a little one's room. This smart space uses extra wide bold stripes in sherbet tints to create a feeling that's as much fun as a circus but as pretty as a spring garden. To keep the look from becoming too sweet, no conventional floral prints were used. Instead, whimsical farm animals and checks lend a fun and frisky air. White wicker furniture has its own woven pattern that contributes subtle interest. What's more, these wicker furniture pieces will retain their charm long after she's outgrown the crib.

Petal Perfect Hooks

WHAT YOU'LL NEED
Transfer paper
Pencil
1-inch-thick plywood
Handheld jigsaw or saber saw
Fine sandpaper
Damp cloth
Drill and drill bit same diameter as wood hook or dowel
Wood glue
Wood hook or dowel
Screwdriver and 1-inch-long screws
Paint and paintbrushes
Picture hanger

1. Using transfer paper, apply pattern to plywood. If pattern is not size you want, enlarge or reduce it on photocopier. Cut out pattern with handheld jigsaw or saber saw, or have pattern cut at a hardware or home supply store. Sand edges smooth, and wipe clean with damp cloth.

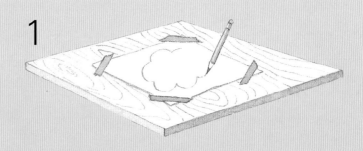

2. Mark center of cutout, and drill hole into wood, stopping about halfway. Wipe clean, then fill hole with wood glue. Insert wood hook or dowel into hole. Wipe away excess glue; let dry.

3. On back of cutout, mark center. Using screwdriver, countersink screw through wood and into dowel or wood hook.

4. Paint cutout as desired; let dry. Following manufacturer's instructions, attach picture hanger to back of cutout, and hang.

White wicker, white sheers, and gauzy white shades all set off the sherbet colors of the room. The colorful valance-and-swag treatment is crisp but doesn't require a lot of fabric. The same fabrics brighten a comfy little chair pillow.

This room leaves lots of open floor space for when baby starts crawling. A fun little lamp repeats the motifs found on the walls and fabrics. You may be able to find such accessories in coordinated groups with wallcoverings and fabrics or make your own with stencils or decoupage. Designer: Diane Holdren, Holdren's Interiors, Inc. Faux finisher/artist: Whitney Brock, Brockworks, Inc.

Let the Games Begin

This spacious, well-planned room may house an infant now, but it will make any little boy feel like a prince for years to come. The fabric and coordinating wallcovering border feature beautifully detailed jousting knights—a motif the room's occupant will still appreciate as he grows up. The handsome wood floor, painted with timeless board games such as backgammon and chess, continues the theme of friendly contest. A nicely designed mix of open and closed built-in storage units makes it easy to keep things neat. It takes planning to create a theme room that doesn't overdo a motif, and this space keeps its balance nicely. Long after the crib has been replaced with a big boy's bed, this room will be a haven fit for a king.

A window gets star treatment with a Roman shade and matching window seat cushion. If your budget doesn't allow for built-ins, you could achieve a similar effect with a sturdy toy chest beneath a window flanked by a freestanding armoire and bookcase. Just be sure to secure the storage pieces to the wall.

Hand-painted and full-size, a Chinese checkerboard brightens up a corner of this little boy's room. A different board game was painted on the floor in each corner. While it may be awhile until he can actually play these games, the design acknowledges that kids spend a lot of their time playing at floor level. Decorative painting: Lucianna Samu and Steven Hammel.

Jousting knights adorn wall borders and fabrics throughout this regal boy's room. Built-in storage and a pelmet (hard valance) pulled out flush with the storage units create a cozy sense of enclosure around a custom window seat. The handsome crib has safely rounded finials. Designer: Ellen Roche, EJR Architects.

95

Sweet Sentiments

Like a cherished photo from a bygone age, this delicately tinted room re-creates a more sentimental time for a baby girl of today. For all its old-fashioned charm, this room is no museum piece. Washable cotton fabrics, vintage furniture, and unfussy accessories make it easy to live with. To create this feminine feeling, start with vintage white furniture and add softly faded, gently ruffled fabrics. Delicate tea roses, those most traditional of flowers, take a starring role, appearing on print fabrics and appliqués as well as in simply framed wall art. Roses are a natural choice for a pink-and-white room, but you could create an equally appealing look with white violets, tiny blue forget-me-nots, or pansies in soft yellow, white, purple, and blue.

A pretty little settee heaped with ruffled pillows is fun for a girl of any age. Shop resale stores for vintage cotton fabrics you can use to upholster new cushions and pillows, or look for new pieces in reproduction prints.

A big built-in hutch with upper storage is an old house fixture, but white paint gives this one a fresh new life. A generously scaled easy chair and ottoman make storytime cozy and comfortable.

Gauzy netting and curtains enhance the dreamy atmosphere of this delicate pastel-tinted room. (Keep curtains out of baby's reach, and remove netting when she starts trying to stand.) Vintage or reproduction, printed cottons are pretty and practical. Designer: Pamela DiCapo. Retailer: Lauren Alexandra.

Cute as a Bunny

Beatrix Potter's beloved Peter Rabbit is the star of this beguiling baby's room. The gentle tales of Peter and his friends Benjamin Bunny, Tom Kitten, and the other denizens of Potter's charming English countryside have appealed to little ones for a hundred years, and they're still going strong. All the detailed charms of Potter's original watercolor illustrations are captured on the wallcovering, and the rich yet delicate hues are picked up in other accents throughout the room. Little ones delight in friendly illustrations such as these, and the allover pattern lets even small tots view them up close and personal. To keep the mostly white room from looking washed out, a rainbow plaid fabric adds punch in a pattern that would work for boys or girls and appeal to older children, too.

A dear little lamp, decorated to coordinate with the Beatrix Potter wallcovering, sheds a gentle light on diaper-changing tasks. As baby grows, you'll need to keep breakable keepsakes and other unsafe items out of his or her reach, but, for now, they're purely charming.

Sleek hardware-free contemporary furniture in a smooth white lacquer finish features rounded edges and corners for safety. United by fresh white, practical contemporary pieces and antique-style accents look perfectly at home together. Lively geometric prints are wonderfully versatile; just change the solid color from pink to blue for a baby boy.

You'll spend a lot of time cuddling baby, so get off your tired feet while you're at it. A great cushy armchair like this one or a rocking chair with a cushioned pad are just what you need. For extra credit, choose a spirited spill-hiding print kids won't outgrow.

One of a Kind

Once upon a time, there were three baby girls whose parents had three very different ideas about decorating. These ideas got a great workout when it came time to create rooms for their daughters. Different as the rooms are, they share some appealing elements. Each features the color pink—that timeless girlhood favorite. Each also includes a distinctive, pretty crib and a comfortable chair with gentle roll arms for cuddly times together. That's where the resemblances end. One room is filled with exuberant romantic flair; another is soothing, sweet, and timelessly traditional; and the third combines nostalgic charm with a funky vintage feeling. Whatever your style, you don't need to buy a complete ready-made furniture set. Furnish your little one's room with unique finds, and your decorating story can end happily, too.

Are these urban loft walls faux or for real? Who cares? The whimsical bed with birdhouse finials and white fence pickets has fun with country icons, and the rumpled chenille chair is agreeably retro. Retailer: The Magic Moon.

Vintage pink and orchid fabrics, layered and pieced together, make this room pretty and expressive. The look appears casual, but it's actually an artful balance: Small areas of intense color and pattern play against large areas of simpler patterns and lighter tints. Designer: Pamela DiCapo. Retailer: Lauren Alexandra.

A muted coral pink warms a quietly charming room that enjoys timeless appeal. The contemporary crib and traditional seating share graceful curves; the old pine cabinet and new checkerboard quilt could have been companions in colonial times. Manufacturer: Waverly.

Curiouser and Curiouser

A nursery designed around the slightly edgy, whimsical world of Alice in Wonderland shows a lively imagination at work—and at play. Hand-painted scenes and characters pay homage to the original spirit of the famous Victorian storybook by Lewis Carroll. The Cheshire Cat, White Rabbit, Mad Hatter, Alice, and other timeless characters adorn the walls, furniture, and ceiling. Even without the hand-painted characters, however, this room is a brilliant play of colors and patterns. Crayon-box stripes, zippy checkerboard and gingham checks, pin dots, and a pretty floral on an ethereal blue ground are just some of the cheerful prints that work charmingly together. The black-and-white accents appeal to even the youngest baby, while the sophisticated mix of prints is one parents will love.

Curvy French country–style furniture gets an extra big jolt of charm with hand painting. The frisky designs combine sharp black-and-white details (easy for babies to see) with popular pastel blues, pinks, and yellows. The result is fresh and delightfully one of a kind.

A large-scale wall mural of the Mad Hatter was clearly this designer's cup of tea, but the masterful treatment would work with just about any children's classic. Hand-painted motifs throughout the room offer lots of visual stimulation; the use of jewel tones and pastels keep the lively mix from over-whelming the look.

Balloon curtains, a "tuffet" footstool with teapot legs, and fabrics in a hip mix of hues will keep their appeal as the room's tiny occupant grows. Designer: Julia Blailock, ASID, Blailock Design.

Newborn Treasures

Today's array of clever, charming furniture and accessory pieces for nurseries make shopping a delight. These days, lively, trendy items are available at all price points to suit the boldest contemporary decorating style. For the traditionalist, there are also more trend-proof, tenderhearted items than ever, because cherishing little ones is timeless. For decorators of either stripe, a wealth of fantasy pieces (and practical pieces dressed up in fantasy garb) creates a style that's strictly kid stuff. And why not? As long as you put safety and comfort first, there's no better place to indulge a cute, creative fantasy or two than in your little dreamer's room.

Delicately antiqued and embellished with a bird's nest, ribbons, and flowery vines, this lovely Old World–inspired crib of American maple is a work of art, just like your little treasure. A piece like this is a family heirloom in the making. Manufacturer: Jane Keltner Designs, Inc.

A rocking chair is a timeless icon of comfort for a baby's room, but it doesn't have to be vintage wood. A roll-arm easy chair with big rockers instead of feet spans traditional and modern style with inviting flair. This is a chair to cuddle baby in every day and night. Retailer: Room & Board.

Picture-book prints from the 1950s are old enough to be sweetly traditional, new enough to be retro and funky. For a hip family with a soft side, prints like this are just right. Find them in the attic or in vintage bookstores, and fit them into softly colored frames. Manufacturer: The Warm Biscuit Bedding Co.

A snug-as-a-bug rug is the perfect accent for baby's room—especially if you want to decorate before you know the baby's gender. Vibrant colors will capture your little one's attention, while the plush surface will provide a soft place to stand while changing diapers or lulling baby to sleep. Manufacturer: PJ Kids.

A garden-theme baby's room would welcome this elegant, versatile changing table/chest with liftoff top and silvery butterfly drawer pulls. Designer: Pam O'Hallaron, ASID. Manufacturer: Bratt Decor, Inc.

Space for Tiny Tots

Little ones who are past the baby stage but not yet grade-school age are what many parents find the most delightful and challenging time of childhood. At this stage, they're mobile, but they aren't aware of dangers. Even if you tell them a dozen times, they have to be on the older side of this age group to remember safety rules. Toddlers and preschoolers are fully engaged with exploring the real world, but the border between what's real and what's imaginary is often blurred in their minds. Their perceptions are developing at

warp speed, so they're often more easily frightened as well as more easily delighted than younger children are. The best rooms for toddlers and preschoolers celebrate the delightful aspects of this magical age. At the same time, they keep up with the challenges posed by curious, active little ones.

Toddlers and preschoolers have a lot in common—especially their energy levels. But there are differences. One of the most important is that toddlers are not really able to appreciate complex visuals. If you have your heart set on elaborate wall murals or other detailed artwork, know up front that you will probably enjoy them well before your little one will. You may opt to wait until your child is a preschooler or even a bit older. On the other hand, you'll be spending a lot of time in your son or daughter's room, so if the decorating scheme makes you happy, that feeling will be communicated to your child.

If you decide to wait until your child is three or four, you can go all out with a favorite storybook theme both of you can enjoy, but you may still want to use a bit of caution. Expensive trompe l'oeil hand-painting rendered on a canvas or board and protected with polyurethane can be enjoyed for awhile and, when it's outgrown, saved for the next generation. If your youngster clamors for some cartoon image you expect will be a temporary thing, you may opt for posters and low-cost pictures. Tape up a few, or spring for colorful, inexpensive frames with clear acrylic instead of glass.

Whether you use hand-painted artworks or low-cost posters, do keep in mind that kids at this age don't know for sure what's real and what's imaginary. Stick with the happy,

We're all more comfortable when a room physically fits the way we function, but when the occupant is a toddler or preschooler, the stakes are much higher. Because they're hardwired to learn about (that is, explore) their world as fast as possible, little ones can be in danger wherever their curiosity takes them, even at home. It's a good idea to accept that physical safety is up for grabs just about all the time with most toddlers, and things only get relatively easier with preschoolers. You can hire a service to come to your home and childproof it or do a little research on your own to learn basic safety precautions. This book lists many of these precautions, but you may also want to "walk through" your space and put yourself at your child's level—literally.

Admittedly, "kidproofing" isn't as much fun as decorating. But the bonus of making your home safe for a toddler or preschooler is that the rest of the family is likely to be safer, too. After all, antiscald devices in showers, nonslip rug pads, and other common-sense tips make sense for everybody, don't they?

gentle aspects of classic nursery rhymes and fairy tales, and exercise even more caution with today's cartoon and movie characters. What may be exciting or merely interesting to a bigger child can be very frightening to a little one, especially if it's on view at bedtime.

Unless you and your child are truly smitten with some motif, you may find, as many parents do, that a design that merely suggests a theme may prove more appealing, longer. A forest, a beach, or another nature scheme is a surefire winner with both girls and boys and can serve as a background for a great variety of imaginative scenarios. Even more versatile is a room scheme based simply on cheerful color combinations and patterns. With this approach, tomorrow's favorite toys and collectibles will fit in as easily as today's. In fact, since most kids don't make a clean break from one phase to the next, an easygoing design based on color will let several eras and enthusiasms coexist peacefully.

Fabric Fair

Pretty, scalloped furniture pieces are the stock in trade of juvenile bedroom groups for girls. But once you've found the necessary bed, dresser, and desk, then what? This beguiling room shows just how much further you can take a look with the right mix of paint and fabrics. The effect is captivating, thanks to a wonderful color palette and loving attention to dressmaker details. A scheme of chartreuse, pink, and white creates a lighthearted ambience. Bigger furniture is off-white with pretty lines; small accessories of knotty pine are enhanced with custom-painted treatments. What's really special is the sprightly mix of simple cotton fabrics and trim. Small-, medium-, and large-scale prints are used lavishly, but they're balanced for visual harmony and united by a shared color scheme. The result? Springtime, year-round.

You don't have to spend a mint to get a charming, creative look as long as you're true to your chosen color scheme. Details on a pretty little desk are picked out in paint, and a simple wood chair gets comfy with plump cushions and cheerful bows.

Full-length curtains get extra punch from contrast-edging and generous trims. A chaise longue in four fabrics and two trims is as artful as the custom-painted floorcloth underfoot. (If you use ball fringe in a young child's room, be sure it's sewn securely onto the fabric.)

Layered lightweight cotton print fabrics give a blithe, countrified air to a charming four-poster bed. Chartreuse teacups form a witty Disneyesque chandelier. Designer: Pamela DiCapo. Retailer: Lauren Alexandra.

The simple coin dots and stripes embellishing these walls are painted, but you could achieve a similar effect with wallcoverings. Little skirted chairs in checks add a layer of visual interest.

Castle Keep

If your youngster is blessed with a good-size bedroom and you've got a connection with some talented craftspeople, the sky's the limit when it comes to imaginative design. This lucky youngster's room is a total fantasy environment. It's practical, too: Just about every medieval castle element leads a double life as a storage unit. To create a similar effect, a good understanding of the historical architectural icons that say "castle" is useful. This is, after all, a little boy's room, where bold and simple shapes work best. Start with a big, kid-friendly idea, plan it out in detail, and you'll have a room memories are made of.

Wood blocks that mimic stone quoins around the arched door, a faux-iron grille made of wood, and charming round turrets give this castle entrance wonderful style. Everything is smoothly finished for safety. Inside, wall-to-wall storage makes neatness easier.

A castle-style storage unit features lots of kid-size drawers plus cubbyholes for fast work of straightening up.

A room-height castle complete with whimsical guards makes this little boy's bedroom a dream come true. A colorful pavilion-style window treatment and appealing trompe l'oeil mural background complete the look with fun and savoir faire. Designer: Mark Wilkinson.

111

Artistic Temperament

If you're the artistic type, chances are your youngsters will share (or at least appreciate) that special sensibility. This exuberant, unconventional room celebrates the fun-loving child who lives here. It also gives a creative parent a chance to indulge some arty impulses. Most of this room's lively patterns were drawn freehand, but some were created with wallpaper and fabric. Remnants, which are very affordable, as well as bigger pieces were enlisted for a fearless medley of patterns. What ties everything together is color. The scheme features a range of hot pastels and slightly "off" primary colors, including aqua, pink, lilac, tomato, chartreuse, and sunflower, but the result isn't chaotic because the chosen hues are repeated. The effect is a sense of happy individuality. What's better than that?

Little friends and big ones alike can enjoy the picnic-party ambience of this playful room. Walls, chairs, and even the ceiling and radiator are decorated with whimsical painted patterns.

A tiny hallway serves as a charming old-fashioned cloakroom when outfitted with coat hooks at several levels. An adjacent staircase features pink sponge-painted rails and an improbable mix of patterns on the stair steps, but, somehow, it all works.

If your child has a colorful collection, why not let it all hang out—literally? A bunch of mostly red handbags makes a fun and funky statement on the wall. Not to mention, it looks cute and keeps dress-up accessories easily at hand.

Fairyland Flair

Cicely Mary Barker's flower fairies spring to life in a little girl's room filled with elfin charm. Ice pink walls and a pale lilac carpet set the stage for a parade of winsome creatures in lovingly rendered backgrounds that give children a fairy's-eye view of the natural world. Adding to the room's timeless charm, Beatrix Potter's world of Peter Rabbit and friends are reproduced on the simple chest of drawers. Richly tinted detailed illustrations stimulate the eyes and brain in a perfectly pleasant way. The spacious room seems even more airy thanks to its simple, uncluttered scheme. Most of the everyday clutter of childhood is neatly stashed behind decorated cupboards and drawers, so there's plenty of room to play and relax. What could be more enchanting?

Old-fashioned cupboards, each decorated with a different flower fairy scene, run floor to ceiling across one whole wall of this little girl's room. It's a masterful approach that provides the room's young occupant with great storage plus a whole world of charming images to enjoy.

Framed by cabinet doors, each watercolor flower fairy scene adds to the charm of this pretty room. A similar effect could be created with another children's series. Less-used toys and clothes are stashed in upper cabinets; everyday favorites are stowed at easy-to-reach levels.

A traditional cottage-style pine bed, farm chest, and nightstand are bathed in a wash of pink so pale the knots in the pine wood show through. It's a look both rustic and tender, one that can take the knocks of childhood while sitting pretty.

Feminine Charms

Wallcoverings and fabrics make it easy to create a lighthearted, girlish look in any bedroom, as these three pretty spaces show. Whether you prefer a clean contemporary palette or a softly antiqued one, pastel florals, stripes, and plaids create simple charm. To give a girlish scheme a little extra substance, ground it with a piece of interesting furniture with good lines, some eye-catching details, and perhaps an heirloom background. In the rooms shown here, that job is done by an elaborately scrolled daybed, a weathered armoire with latticed doors, and a roomy upholstered chair in an antique print. Pieces like these have staying power that can last until your girl heads off to college and can be just as charming in a guest room later.

Teddy bears first won our hearts more than a century ago, and few childhood icons have proved as popular with both boys and girls. Coordinating wallpaper and fabric patterns let you celebrate the "bear" essentials throughout your child's room. Manufacturer: Brewster Wallcovering Co.

A French-style daybed gets an even more romantic look with a white gauze canopy. Flower-sprigged Roman shades and a coordinating carpet extend the airy look. Built-in storage shelves around the window makes a pretty room practical. Designer: Susann Kelly Interiors.

Simple details enrich the look of a little one's bedroom. A whimsical bed skirt is easy to put on and take off thanks to bows looped over simple round knobs. The door gate is a charming detail that's also functional, keeping your child out of the adjacent play area during naptime. Retailer: The Magic Moon.

Step Right Up

The circus has always been a popular theme for a child's room, but this interpretation is more dramatic and sophisticated than most. A masterful mural that ranges around the room is an extraordinary piece of art that doesn't rely on bright colors for its drama. Befitting the rich, relatively quiet palette, the furniture is also something special. A fusion of Craftsman, Asian, and modern styles, these pieces are strikingly handsome yet sturdy enough for active kids. If you appreciate the timeless, resilient appeal of classic wood, metal, and cloth toys, you'll find it satisfying to furnish your treasured little one's room with the same kind of heirloom quality. Years from now, you'll still be glad you did. Your child and grandchild might be glad, too!

Simple yet comfortable, this desk and chair withstand fidgety, climbing kids in style. The wonderful mural is stimulating without being visually overwhelming. Big, round drawer pulls are easy for youngsters to grasp, and they're safer than metal pulls, too.

Barn red, slate blue, and tawny brown shades leap from the walls onto the room's furnishings. If you can't find furniture like this, Mission or contemporary wood pieces can give you a similarly rustic yet graceful effect. Designer: Mark Wilkinson.

Garden Bright

Fresh-picked charm abounds in this lively room, thanks to a lime and aqua color scheme that can please your girl for a long time. With the exception of a few floral graphic treatments, this is not a flowery space. Plaids and checks in frisky tints create a look that's feminine but cool and sporty at the same time. The room takes a casual tongue-in-cheek approach to garden style, with amusing results. A few giant flowers on the walls and floor, larger-than-life dragonflies at the window, and window boxes filled with whimsical wooden blooms set the stage with charm. A surprising mix of wicker and leather-upholstered furniture adds punch to this confident, cheerful space.

A fun yet subtle graphic of giant flowers is in good company next to oversize dragonfly tiebacks. But it's the kicky pint-size armchairs in berry- and lime-colored leather that really give this room its one-of-a-kind flair. Designer: Terri Ervin, INTERIORS by Decorating Den.

This large walk-in closet under the eaves makes a charming playroom hideaway adjacent to the pretty bedroom. Its orchid and periwinkle tints are a perfect complement to the yellow-green bedroom. Real window boxes filled with florist's moss set up the surprise of fancifully painted wood flowers.

Girlhood Charm

A pastel palette of the lightest greens, pinks, yellows, and blues—all frosted in white—gives these bedrooms a gentle feminine feeling. A closer look, however, shows that these spaces have been planned with the needs of active young girls in mind. Furniture is scaled for little ones, beds are free of pointed posts or other dangerous elements, and there's plenty of storage for all her favorite things. What's more, while the look is undeniably girlish and delicate, it's not overly fragile. Patchwork and checked fabrics, knotty pine that's been painted and distressed, and nostalgic accents all contribute to a sturdy country look. You'll find cute pieces like these in ready-to-finish furniture stores and resale shops as well as kids' specialty retailers.

A house-shape bed with a cubbyhole/dollhouse footboard is charming, cozy, and very clever. Built-in bookcases flanking a graceful window seat offer a creative way to make the most of every inch. Designer: Pamela DiCapo. Retailer: Lauren Alexandra.

When you want a change from wood furniture without sacrificing traditional appeal, consider wicker or rattan. These pretty, white-painted charmers evoke the romance of a Victorian porch at teatime. Seat cushions with big crisp bows add the perfect finish. Designer: Pamela DiCapo. Retailer: Lauren Alexandra.

A daisy-top table, an Adirondack chair, a bed skirt trimmed with ball fringe, and other charming old-fashioned elements help create nostalgic appeal in this room. A mirror inset into a cupboard door gives the piece extra versatility. Designer: Pamela DiCapo. Retailer: Lauren Alexandra.

Princess in Residence

Pink ruffled curtains are a familiar sight in little girls' rooms, but that's just the beginning in this marvelous space. On the walls, murals feature magical ponies and ballroom swags, and the ceiling's rosette is embellished with faux tassels. Within the room, beautifully made wood furnishings blur the line between furniture and theater. Each piece is thoughtfully designed to evoke fairy tale ideas, but each is also crafted for simplicity and safety. While white furniture is a popular choice for young girls' rooms, this room shows that's not always necessary to create a feminine feeling. Paired with pink, rosy red, and gold, the warmth of natural wood has its own allure. In the right hands, it's downright magical.

A pretty little vanity and coordinating chair are sturdy and smooth for the safety of little ones. Heart and crown shapes carry the mood with the simplicity suited to this age group.

A ceiling-height castle is beautifully detailed for maximum charm. Periwigged mice, rose trees, and other familiar fairy tale icons bring this piece to life. Inside, it's a well-planned storage unit for toys and clothes.

Recalling Cinderella's enchanted pumpkin turned coach, this marvelous little nest cuddles a young lady in comfort and style. Special touches include a castle scene painted on the interior and an exterior bench for the froggy driver. Designer: Mark Wilkinson.

Collecting with Charm

This little girl's family is into collections, and it's a sure bet the hobby will be passed on in style. The spacious room abounds in nostalgic decorating elements. Some are truly old, others are new pieces inspired by vintage styles, and all convey a sense of charm and comfort. In one corner, a quaint 1930s quilt featuring sunbonnet babies covers a vintage white iron-and-brass bed. In another, a built-in desk is crowned with shelves filled with family mementos and photos. In still another corner, a traditionally styled armoire gets a fresh look with chicken wire inserts and hand-painted decorations. Individual accessories are interesting, yet the overall look isn't choppy: The whole space is unified with a cameo pink background that's as soothing as a lullaby.

Long after the kiddy table and chairs are outgrown, the white Victorian wicker desk chair and built-in work space will keep on performing beautifully. Open shelves make it easy to enjoy inspiring mementos and keep things neat.

Small children and small objects don't mix, so these smart parents kept cute collections out of harm's way with a high wall-mounted display cabinet. The open shelves are just deep enough for one layer of collectibles; the scalloped edge lightens the look.

A hand-painted armoire decorated with a chicken wire inset, sponge painting, and floral stencils turns necessary storage into a pretty focal point. A confection of ruched Austrian shades frames the view with feminine appeal. Designer: Janet Lohman Interior Design.

A deep closet converted to a feature-filled playhouse would delight any child. The first floor includes open storage shelves and a charming tea table area; a ladder-accessed second story adds more storage space and plenty of room to play. Decorative painting: Lucianna Samu and Steven Hammel.

Cheerful Charm

A tree house doesn't have to be rustic, as the one in this pretty room shows. This tree house owes its inspiration to a storybook cottage or dollhouse. The bedroom's overall scheme gives an airy garden style an especially lighthearted twist with sunny yellow and hot pink. Tailored plaid fabrics keep these sherbet hues from becoming too sweet. The playhouse area is carved out of a recessed closet and embellished with realistic shingles and siding. It's filled with storage features plus comfy places to play make-believe or curl up with a book. Underscoring the garden cottage motif, simple small-scale furniture pieces get a special look with hand-painted flowers. A vintage metal bed with distressed white paint furthers the airy look.

Hot-pink-and-yellow plaid makes a cheery counterpoint to a winsome, mostly white background. The flowerpot-motif wallpaper is cute but not visually obtrusive. A small curio cabinet keeps a precious collection of Madame Alexander dolls stashed safely but visibly. Designer: Ellen Roche, EJR Architects.

Surprising Sophisticate

This room is filled with charming elements to beguile a very young girl, but a second glance reveals a sophisticated plan that will keep its appeal as she grows. Architecturally, the room is spectacular, with big graceful windows, beautifully crafted built-in storage, a fine wood floor, and lots of space. Even without all those attributes, however, the room would shine, thanks to an artful decorating scheme. Rosy red and ivory lend a cheerful air that's not too sweet. Because colors tend to blend in the eye, this red-and-white framework welcomes all tints of pink, from powder to raspberry to burgundy. White and other neutrals plus tints and shades of a favorite color can work equally well. It's a simple formula that can be fun and sophisticated, too.

A curved pelmet (hard valance) bridges two tall built-in storage units and adds a cozy alcove feeling to this window seat. A crisp plaid cushion gives the pink-and-white scheme a tailored edge.

Lavishly gathered Roman shades in a wonderful ruby-and-ivory floral stripe have a ball gown look that appeals to all ages. So does the subtle blush-and-white-stripe wallcovering. A little table and skirted chairs and a pretty bed decorated with garland have pint-size appeal. Designer: Ellen Roche, EJR Architects.

Diamonds are forever when they make a lustrous wood floor even more beautiful. This subtle design pairs two pale neutrals sparked with small diamond shapes in a rosewood hue. Perimeter stripes create the look of a bordered rug. Decorative painting: Lucianna Samu and Steven Hammel.

131

Ribbons and Roses

If you want to concoct a cute room for a little girl but don't want it to go out of style before she's halfway grown, consider the classics. Garlands of roses and pink ribbon bows have been feminine favorites for ages, and their appeal is still going strong. This room, decorated with these timeless motifs, shows just how perennial that appeal is. To keep the pink-and-white scheme from feeling chilly, walls are treated to a creamy custard yellow. Small yellow accents, including bows scattered on the pink-and-white comforter, repeat the sunny hue. Some of the white furniture is decorated with flowers and bows, but most of it is left unadorned. With a bit of restraint, your frilly look will stay fresh.

A charming mix of three soft pink-and-white prints gives this room subtle liveliness. The balance of beribboned, striped, and floral prints was carefully worked out for a harmonious look, with the airiest, simplest print used the most. Designer: Suzanne S. Curtis, ASID.

For a unifying fresh effect, all the furniture in this little girl's room is painted white. A kid-size coat tree is practical for children too young to cope with hangers and closets.

133

Play Zones Ahead

A custom-built platform cleverly hides an abundance of floor-level storage in shallow drawers. In the background, a delicately tinted scene features some favorite childhood's storybook characters. A low bookcase makes a simple, practical headboard.

Too much space for a kid's room is not a common problem, but even a smaller room could benefit from the savvy ideas found in this unusually large play-and-sleep suite. Most obvious is the charming perspective-bending mural that decorates one whole wall and extends via the famous yellow brick road down into the room itself. Equally exciting is the playful "grassy" platform that curves through the space. It creates a comfortable, safe base for a mattress, and the low, shallow drawers built into the platform make it easy for children to put things away. Sliding screens are another smart idea; they provide lots of space for drawing pictures and playing school. No "don't touch" rules apply here—it's all about fun and freedom! Who says a safe learning environment can't be cool?

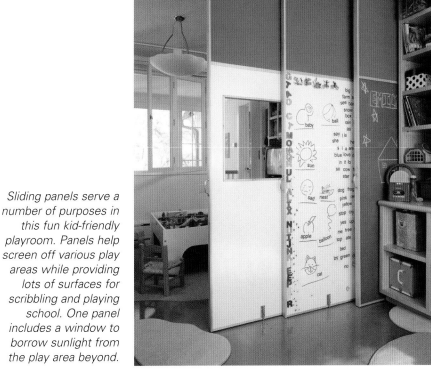

Sliding panels serve a number of purposes in this fun kid-friendly playroom. Panels help screen off various play areas while providing lots of surfaces for scribbling and playing school. One panel includes a window to borrow sunlight from the play area beyond.

A platform, carpeted in soft spring green, extends its grassy look up nearby walls. Custom carpeting in curving shapes leads the eye and visually breaks up the unusually large space.

Fairy-Tale Forest

An enchanted forest figures importantly in many beloved fairy tales, so it's no wonder stepping into this room evokes a magical feeling. A glorious mural, depicting castles, mountains, wildflower fields, and garland-twined trees, runs ceiling to floor around the entire room. Against this background, an armoire out of *Beauty and the Beast*, a Goldilocks bed, and other charming elements make this space a dream come true for an imaginative youngster. The room has been decorated to please a girl, but, with a change of bedding, window treatments, and rugs, it would work just as well for a budding Robin Hood. Well-constructed wood furniture is key: It's got the timeless charm you'd expect to find in a storybook cottage, but it's sturdy enough for real life today.

A cottage-style chair cozies up to a well-made little vanity that's pretty but not pretentious. A wicker hamper stashes dirty clothes in style. Behind it all, the wonderful mural extends the magical mood around the room.

A pretty, Gothic-style window gets the royal treatment from a lavish swag festooned with bows and a rosette, but the use of simple checked fabric keeps the mood light. A wicker trunk makes a safe lightweight toy box. Designer: Mark Wilkinson.

A wall becomes a play surface when areas are covered in Velcro hook and loop fasteners; little cars can be attached. A washable bedspread with yellow and checkerboard motifs is clever and practical. Even the bedside "stoplight" carries the theme. Designer: Julia Dutton Haidlen, ASID, J. Haidlen Design Associates. Architect: Scott Meyers, DelValle Homes.

Raring to Go

Lots of little guys are crazy for vehicles—especially race cars. If you've got car-loving kids at home, why not indulge them? This room's winning formula starts with primary colors plus black and white—all eye-catching colors with proven kid appeal. Then, it features an array of race car motifs to spark added excitement. Each area of the room carries the theme to triumph. For example, a ho-hum view didn't stop the action: An over-the-top valance uses bright high-contrast colors and dashing shapes to give kids plenty to look at. An ordinary wall is transformed into fun topography that adds visual interest but actually works as a miniature "roadway." A few big gestures like these makes a dramatic difference in how a room looks.

Race Car Valance

WHAT YOU'LL NEED

Tape measure
Approximately 2 yards fabric
Scissors
Sewing machine
Iron and ironing board
Synthetic fiber
Pins
Approximately 2 yards polyester quilt batting, ½ inch thick
Craft glue
Staple gun and staples

1. Measure cornice you want to cover. Width of fabric piece for valance should equal front facing of cornice width plus widths of both sides plus 6 inches. For fabric height, measure height of front facing and add 4 inches.

2. To cover cornice, sew together race-car-theme fabrics to create desired pattern. To make checkerboard points, cut 12 to 16 triangles from fabric. Each triangle should be about 7 inches long and 6 inches at its widest point. With right sides facing, stitch each triangle together, leaving straight bottom edge open. Turn and press, then lightly stuff each with synthetic fiber. Center triangles along bottom edge of fabric for front facing. With right sides facing and raw edges aligned, stitch points in place.

3. Affix quilt batting over front and sides of cornice with craft glue. When dry, stretch fabric taut so it's aligned with cornice board and checkerboard points hang from bottom edge. Wrap fabric edges around to back of board; staple fabric in place. To cover top, stretch fabric over dust board. Wrap fabric edges around to back of dust board, and staple in place. Continue smoothing and stapling until fabric lies flat. Mount cornice.

The view outside this bedroom is of a neighbor's wood fence, but that doesn't matter a bit when the window valance is this exciting. A 3-D valance of colorful race car brands is bordered with checkerboard flag points that almost flutter in the raceway wind.

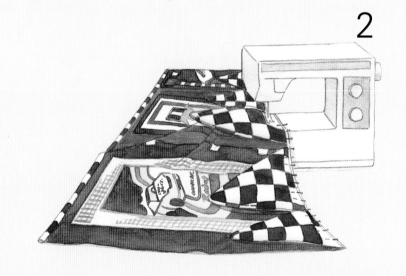

2

Colorful Chic

Melon and yellow with accents of green make not only a pretty scheme but one with enough dash to last when your little girl gets bigger. The same concept would work with turquoise and white plus coral, periwinkle and white plus sunflower, or another combination that appeals to you. The key is to pair hot pastels that are more sophisticated than the usual red/blue/yellow primary scheme and gutsier than pale baby blue and pink. Then, just add generous amounts of white for instant freshness. Hot pastels give today's active, confident girls a look they can enjoy without giving up their sweeter side. Look for room-making prints that deliver a casual, contemporary twist on floral motifs, and you've got a look that's chic and charming.

Ruched and gathered lining fabric goes from nice to fabulous with a lavishly gathered rosette above the canopied bed. Dressmaker details like this take a little planning and work, but they'll help keep the room attractive as your girl grows up.

Bed curtains in a cheerful floral stripe update a classic look with contemporary flair. The same print embellishes a cute little cupboard; the white blossoms from the print are hand-painted onto a mirror hung at toddler height for now.

A ruffled Roman shade in striking fabrics gives a pretty window star treatment and establishes the room's color scheme. The kneehole for a desk isn't needed for homework yet, so a simple gathered curtain turns it into an easy-access hideaway.

Time to Change

Toddlers are all about change, and their rooms need to keep up with their development in a fun, safe way. The two biggest changes for kids in this age group are likely to be the end of diapers and the move out of the crib. A crib that converts to a toddler bed or conventional twin bed is helpful. So is a changing table that can become a chest of drawers or storage shelving unit. Beyond these basics, celebrate creativity (yours and theirs). Charming preschooler-size tables and chairs encourage coloring and crafts as easily as tea parties or snacks; whimsical drawer and cabinet door pulls add an artful finishing touch. A room that's safe yet stimulating is just right.

Putting things away will be great fun with these whimsical chests. Even kids who don't like to eat their veggies will love stashing stuff in this supersize carrot. The other piece shows a lot of attitude, with every drawer awry and arms akimbo. Putting things in this chest will be like child's play! Manufacturer: Straight Line Designs Inc.

A comfortable crib that converts into a pretty bed is a winsome focal point for a charming little girl's room. Bas-relief flower garlands add a dash of romance to a simple bed with safely rounded corners. Manufacturer: Carey More Designs.

Whimsically designed pulls in hand-painted resin or "jewel" studded pewter add a lively, fun look to drawers and cabinet doors. Use them to pick up a color scheme or reinforce a visual theme. Pull collections feature whimsical bugs, sports balls, tea party elements, vehicles, and more. Manufacturer: PJ Kids. Retailer: Bombay Kids (pewter pulls).

Confident and colorful, this wonderfully decorated toddler table and chairs bring the look of art furniture home for everyday enjoyment. Imaginative designs like this play into almost any color scheme. Designer: Meg O'Halloran. Manufacturer: Smellybottoms.com.

You don't need a lot of decorative accessories in an active child's room: Practical everyday items like this giraffe mirror and flowered storage bin can add to the fun and style. Just a few pieces can carry a color scheme and a visual theme. Designer: Diana Cuyler. Manufacturer: Lilypads.

Grade-schoolers' Getaways

Between about age six and 11, children can experience the world in a wonderfully free way. Liberated from the limitations and frustrations of early childhood but not yet in the thick of the demands and concerns of adolescence, kids, in what classic psychology calls the "latency period," are avidly discovering their world and their own potential. You can guide and support this discovery process by the way you design your child's room.

Grade-schoolers are a mixed bag. Like younger kids, they still need space to play on the floor and kick up their heels in safety. But like older kids, they have to contend with a lot of homework. A good-size desk, a comfortable chair, and a min-

imum of breakable knickknacks help satisfy both the big and little kid inside your grade-schooler.

When it comes to decorating the space, a grade-schooler is old enough to have significant input. No guarantees, but the more your child is involved in helping plan the room scheme, the likelier it is he or she will take pride in the space and take care of it. Kids this age often have hobbies, interests, or talents that are already part of their self-definition, so by all means reinforce those you feel are positive.

Keep your eyes open for key items that will pull a positive room concept together for your child. It may be easier than you think. One lively boy who loved the big cats but not his pale turquoise walls changed his mind when given a dramatic quilt depicting a rare white tiger with turquoise eyes. The quilt border colors were turquoise, brown, white, and green, so the rest of the room took on a jungle theme. An artistic girl who had a hard time choosing one or two colors for her room found happiness with a rainbow motif. People began giving her rainbow-decorated accessories, so her room came together quickly. A nice plus: Just about any clear, solid color fits in. What theme can you use to knit together your child's preferences and interests with the room and furnishings you already have?

At this stage of the game, you and your child may still clash on the issue of color, but a grade-schooler is also old enough to understand (or at least accept) your explanation. If he wants vivid blue and bright orange, for example, you can

or an upholstered computer chair. Save the brighter, lighter color for pillows and other small accents. If your child's scheme is navy and yellow, for example, you can swap the yellow for red, light green, pink, or any number of other choices when their tastes change without a big investment.

What if your child's favorite colors and preferred theme seem at odds? If that happens (it may, if you've got a particularly imaginative youngster), look beyond the prepackaged ideas out there. For example, a butterfly theme doesn't have to be delicate and pastel; the common monarch butterfly is dramatic black and orange. So, imagine a room with peach walls hung with monarch butterfly prints and black lacquer furniture with brass butterfly drawer pulls. You get the idea. Virtually any concept can be used with a little creativity.

Stumped on how to make it work? Ask your child. To a grade-schooler, the world of imagination is still clear and present, and a sea green giraffe may be just what he or she had in mind.

satisfy that desire with small furniture items and accents in those hues and treat the walls to a pale room-expanding tint of light blue or light orange sherbet.

Whether you and your child are inspired by a specific theme or just a color scheme, don't feel you have to create something elaborate. Keep in mind that the pictures you see in this book or in decorating magazines are settings at their "company best." In everyday life, a grade-schooler's toys, books, homework projects, and clothes tend to take over all but the most rigorously policed spaces. Even a minimally decorated room will look plenty busy most of the time, so keep it simple.

One proven, simple approach is to develop a color scheme of two or three hues and stick with it when buying or refurbishing pieces. If you have less-than-pedigreed furniture, paint pieces one color and add wood pulls and knobs in another color or design. If you're buying fabric accessories, use the more sedate color for big items such as a comforter

Out of This World

For a youngster who's fascinated by all things astrological, this bedroom really goes all out. The space shuttle effect is virtually perfect, thanks to intense research and attention to a zillion telling little details. At the same time, the room has its down-to-earth aspects. There's storage, a bed, a small combination desk/nightstand, and more. What's most interesting, however, is that traditional room elements are preserved throughout the room. Most of the spaceship effects are created by large-scale photo-realistic wall treatments and small easily removable furniture items. The adjoining bath is treated in the same fashion: Classic traditional elements are permanent, while the novelty futuristic elements are removable. When the young astronaut moves on to other interests, the room can change without calling in the rehabbers.

A traditional six-panel door gets a lift with reflective insets and metallic accents. Faux wires jump the traditional chair rail and link the upper scene with the "controls" below.

A sink cabinet with dentil molding and reeded column details couldn't be more traditional, but the gleaming chrome accessories and spaceship decals carry out the suite's futuristic theme.

Aluminum-face reflective fabric, designed for the space program to retain body heat, is cleverly used as bedding. Dramatic photo-realistic scenes are affixed to the ceiling as well as to the walls, enhancing the space travel feeling.

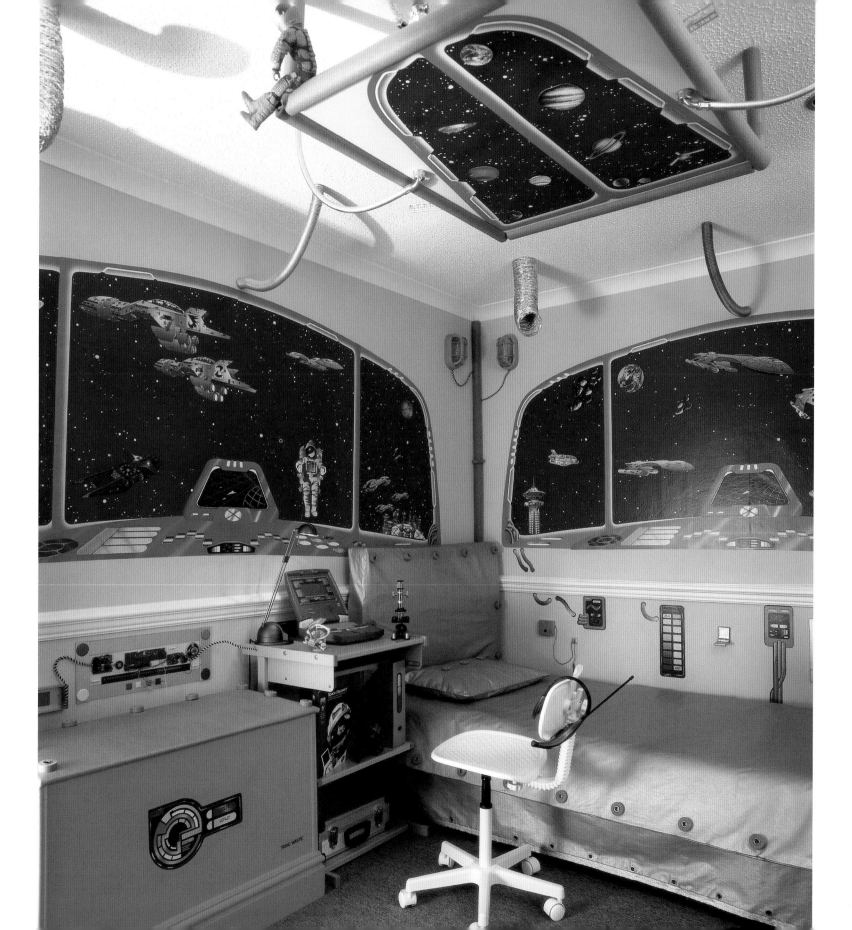

Diamonds, hand-painted on the wall and sewn into a luxurious quilt, create a subtly dynamic feeling. Frogs, a firefly-shape vanity lamp, topiaries, and an outdoor carriage lamp create a witty garden ambience. Designer: Diane Holdren, Holdren's Interiors, Inc.

Garden District

A charming take on garden style, this room owes a bit of inspiration to the French-infused look of New Orleans or Savannah. While many garden schemes for girls use more obvious ice cream tints, this room's chic color scheme is grounded in subtle sage and celery greens. These go-with-everything tints appeal to more sophisticated tastes and look great with periwinkle and mauve. The real stars of the room, however, are the wonderful hand-painted images that embellish walls, trim, and even the bed's headboard. They're whimsical without being too sweet, so they won't be outgrown too quickly. Against this background, pale furniture with hand-painted garden accents really shine. A few amusing accents, such as lengths of white picket fence, complete a garden space with perennial appeal.

What appears to be a freestanding headboard is really traditional recessed paneling trimmed with crown and rope moldings. The subtle hand-painted decorations in tints of green, ivory, and periwinkle lend a lighthearted elegance she'll love for many years to come.

Wonderful hand-painted garden designs give a large door great visual interest. A hand-painted kid-scale table and chairs carry the color scheme; an iron birdbath lamp recalls romantic old cities renowned for their gardens.

On the Frontier

Cowboy style was always a lure for boys, but the American Girl doll phenomenon has popularized frontier lore for girls, too. Today, both boys and girls can find themselves in rustic, easy-to-live-with frontier style, and, if you enjoy country style or collect Americana, it's easy to bring the look to kids' spaces. Many Shaker- and Early American–style furnishings are perfect for children's rooms because these designs are so simple and practical. For example, wall racks with pegs for clothing were frontier fixtures, and they're much easier for kids to use than hangers in closets. Contoured wood chairs are sturdy and comfortable, quilts are colorful and washable, and frontier-style heirlooms are already weathered and faded. And if you find yourself stuck for a color scheme, all–American red, white, and blue is a natural.

Bandanna-print rugs and retro cowboy memorabilia give a boy's room a look that's warm as well as fun. New and vintage elements, united in their color scheme, work seamlessly together. Manufacturer: The Warm Biscuit Bedding Co.

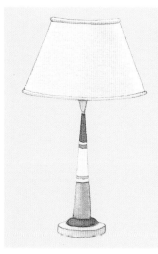

Bright Ideas

Virtually any object can be made into a lamp. The easiest way to do this is to purchase a lamp kit at a hardware or home supply store. This kit will include electrical wiring, foundation supports, and a harp for holding a lamp shade.

Begin by finding a base to match your decor. Clay pots, glass hurricane shades filled with buttons or shells, tightly woven baskets, pottery, and wooden items all work well. If the item is not hollow, drill a hole wide enough for electrical wiring to thread through. Assemble the lamp parts as indicated in the diagram, beginning at the base of the lamp and working up to the socket. Top with a coordinating shade, and voilà! You have an instant conversation piece.

Your not-so-little house in the big woods is the perfect place to create a frontier-style nest for a plucky girl. Flannel sheets and quilts are cozy and easy to care for; an array of vintage pillows and accessories add one-of-a-kind charm. Stylist: Joetta Moulden.

Components of Fun

Fun, flexible, free-spirited, and fuss-free: That's all the best of modern style, and it's all here. This room for a young boy is hard-working and great-looking, too. Rather than focusing on one theme, this room lets its young occupent keep all his favorite treasures around, from superheroes to dinosaurs to trains. What helps keep the room from looking too cluttered is storage—and lots of it. Open storage is a smart solution, and, in this room, it's also an attractive one. Furniture is smooth Finnish birch plywood, but the principles could be applied to virtually any material, from unpeeled cedar logs to laminate. What's key is the focus on providing kids with just what they need for sleep, study, storage, self-expression—and good old-fashioned play.

This combination drawer and open shelf storage unit makes maximum use of space. The corkboard panel offers a place to keep homework and schedules in sight. Making use of an often wasted space, the electric train running around the room's perimeter adds to the fun.

Intensely colorful bed linens and imaginative artwork give this soothing neutral room a jolt of excitement. The neat berthlike bed houses lots of storage or a trundle bed for sleepovers on roll-out casters. Designer: Alla Kazovsky. Manufacturer: Kids' Studio.

Open storage is the easiest to take care of, especially for youngsters, but you don't have to settle for everyday bookcases or plastic bins. This room's storage components create a dynamic, visually appealing architecture.

153

Room to Grow

A room furnished only with a computer desk and a dresser was begging for romantic additions to make it a pretty nest for a young girl. With the purely practical furniture already in place, the homeowner's attention turned to creating a breezy garden-inspired getaway. While this room isn't skimpy, the design devices used here would work miracles in any small room. Sky blue walls give the room an airy feeling that's enhanced by the graceful tall window on one wall. A wonderful trompe l'oeil garden mural visually expands the room even further. Incredibly, the mural isn't an expensive hand-painted one; it's actually wallpaper. The space-expanding approach extends to the floor with the use of an eye-catching rug laid on a diagonal. The result is a cool, comfortable space that can go the distance.

A mix of raspberry stripes, yellow checks, and pink-and-yellow parrot tulip fabrics creates a cheerful, feminine look the occupant won't outgrow. Mixing geometrics with florals is a proven way to create visual interest; just be sure at least one fabric unites the colors of the others.

Roses and daisies are pretty but predictable—not what this homeowner wanted for a special daughter. Pink-and-yellow parrot tulips give a slightly exotic, free-spirited feeling that's more sophisticated yet still garden-casual.

A simple slatted bed and a cushy full-size armchair plus ottoman give this girl's room comfort to spare, without a lot of fuss. Designer: Connie Thompson, INTERIORS by Decorating Den.

That Sporting Life

If you've got a youngster who's an avid sports fan or active player, you can't miss with a room designed around his or her athletic passions. Sports themes have always been popular for boys, and the classic look of these rooms, done up in neutrals and primary hues, shows the timeless versatility of this approach. These days, however, you can also find sportif ensembles for girls in feminine aqua and lilac as well as the usual gray, blue, tan, and red. If your youngster isn't set on particular colors, consider adopting the two-color scheme of a professional or college team your family follows. Unlike many other youthful enthusiasms, a love of sports may last, and you'll have yourself a winning formula for decorating.

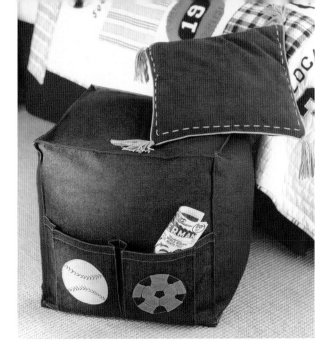

An ottoman is a good idea; an ottoman covered in sturdy denim, accented with fun appliqués and roomy pockets is a great idea! Pieces like this make any kids' room more comfortable and give a big style boost, too.

Handsome traditional furniture doesn't look at all fussy in this lively boy's room. A rich blue background plus colorful, fun accessories give a vibrant feeling. Corkboard offers plenty of room to hang personal paperwork without creating clutter. Retailer: Bombay Kids.

Any young player or fan would warm up to a sports-embellished quilt set like this one. The athletic motif is carried out on a cozy rug, curtains, and more in a color scheme that's rich but not jarring. Retailer: Bombay Kids.

Everything Shipshape

Children often set sail in their imaginations, but it's a rare bedroom that caters to their sea-faring fantasies. This kids' bedroom for two does so, going way beyond the usual bunk bed solution. Sleeping quarters are stacked to save floor space, but the configuration looks for all the world like berths in a ship's stateroom. The delightful effect, snug yet exotic, would please boys and girls alike. Many fantasy environments for kids require a lot of space to realize the effect. Not this one. A ship's stateroom is space-conserving by nature, with under-the-bed and built-in storage common. For accessories, you may find just the right treasures among your last vacation's souvenirs. If not, local import shops offer Asian silks, African carvings, Caribbean shells, and many other finds, often quite affordably.

A brass-rimmed round window that evokes a ship's porthole gives even an ordinary backyard view a slightly foreign feeling. A simple curtain in jewel tones and earthy neutrals adds to the exotic impression.

One great bonus of these cleverly designed berths is that each child has a space to tape up personal masterpieces and other mementos. The upper berth also features a shallow shelf that's far enough down the wall that it doesn't pose a head-bumping hazard.

Curvy vintage furniture gets a fresh new look when it's painted sherbet pink. Whimsical yet sophisticated fabrics are shirred and pleated for extra interest. Installing the Roman shade and bed canopy flush with the ceiling makes the room look taller and each element more dramatic. Designer: Kathryne Dahlman, Kathryne Designs.

High-Flying Fun

If you can't imagine a young girl's room without pink but you're bored with the usual flowery motifs, take inspiration from this sunny space. Instead of floral designs, the room uses a fabric printed with whimsical watercolors of birds. A second print featuring Easter egg–inspired circles and a third in gingham add more lighthearted charm. Sherbet-stripe walls underscore the melon pink, yellow, and pale green scheme. If you're having trouble finding unusual patterns in ready-made curtains, comforter covers, and the like, investigate fabric stores or workrooms that specialize in upholstering and drapery fabrication. They're likely to have a wider range of choices, including coordinating fabric collections for kids created by famous-name designers. The result can be a room that's as sweet and sophisticated as your favorite girl.

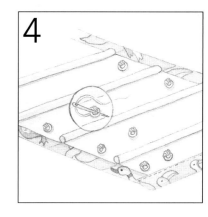

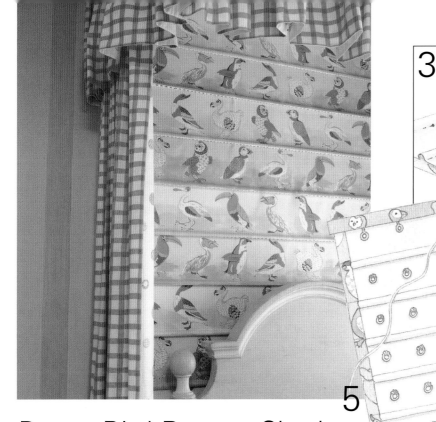

Pretty Bird Roman Shade

WHAT YOU'LL NEED

Tape measure
Shade fabric and lining cut to specified size
Sewing machine
Matching thread
Scissors
Iron and ironing board
Washable fabric marker
Straight pins
Needle
¾-inch plastic curtain rings, 4 for each casing
2-inch-wide piece wood, 1 inch thick, cut to size
Hammer and small brads or nails
Eyelets, 1 for each column of curtain rings
Heavy string or cord (8 times length of finished shade)
½-inch-thick dowels cut to size, 1 for each casing
2 L-brackets, 2 inches each

1. Measure area to be covered horizontally, and add 1 inch. Add 1 inch to vertical measurement for each fold you want shade to have plus 5 inches for hem. (Most shades have folds spaced no more than 6 inches apart.) Purchase and cut out fabric and lining based on measurements.

2. With right sides facing and raw edges aligned, sew fabric and lining together. Trim seams, turn, and press seams flat. Slipstitch opening closed.

3. To make casings for dowels, mark shade on each side at first fold line. With fabric lying flat, fold shade at this line so wrong sides are facing. Pin in place, then stitch 1 inch from fold across shade. Repeat at all fold lines.

4. Lay blind flat with wrong side up. Mark placement of outside curtain rings halfway between each stitched casing line and 1 inch from each side. Mark placement of 2 additional columns of rings, evenly spaced from outside rings. Stitch rings to back of blind.

5. Fold top edge of shade over wood; nail in place. Screw eyelets into underside of wood at top of each column of curtain rings. Cut 4 pieces of cord twice the length of blind. Tie end of 1 piece to curtain ring at bottom of shade in 1 column, and thread loose end up through every ring in same column, then through eyelet. Repeat for each column of rings. Slip dowels through casings.

6. Fasten shade to window or wall with L-brackets. Pull cords taut, and knot together at ends.

Southwestern Savvy

Cowboy motifs are a fixture of a traditional American childhood, but few Wild West–theme rooms are as delightful as this one. Young cowboys and cowgirls alike would warm to this spirited, colorful space. Everywhere you look, there's another amusing take on cowpoke style. Bandanna red and denim blue fabrics are key; the multicolor print of cowboy boots is a fun plus. Whatever style you're creating, appropriate fabrics can go a long way. The best idea in this room may be the creative use of an overhanging eave as a mural focal point. If there's an awkward architectural feature in your child's room, you may find it's easier to exploit it than to hide it. In this case, it's certainly a lot more fun!

A small alcove, no wider than a traditional six-over-six window, becomes a snuggly spot for reading or strumming a cowboy tune. Real bandannas make fun tiebacks for denim blue curtains.

Plain white walls suggest adobe and set off the room's many decorative accents that beguile the eye. The faux divided lite window framed in barn red is really a mirror that visually expands the space.

A big awkward eave is transformed into a dramatic canopy-style headboard thanks to a colorful mural. The moonstruck coyote is a classic Southwestern motif; the horseshoe-embellished iron bed is a master stroke. A fun cowboy boot pattern on the baseboard is repeated on the bed skirt, throw pillows, and valance. Designer: Delia Spradley, Spradley Interiors. Sylist: Joetta Moulden.

Old World Enchantment

The young girl who lives here loves pink and yellow, but her mother didn't want an overly bright treatment her daughter would tire of quickly. The solution was to use romantic, subtle versions of the favored hues: porcelain pink, mauve, antique ivory, and old gold. The girl's existing furniture, simple whitewashed pine with a French country feeling, worked nicely in the space. A simple swagged fabric treatment makes the bed a focal point; a few special vintage pieces, such as the faux bamboo end table and the circus rocking horse, enhance the nostalgic ambience. Delicate trompe l'oeil fairies, leaves, and vines embellish the walls but with a subtle touch. This is a space she'll cherish, now and through the years.

A simple knotty pine desk and hutch, whitewashed so the knots show through, is decorated with a few delicate flower-and-garland accents in watercolor tints. In the corners of the room, watercolor fairies play among the leaves of trompe l'oeil branches.

An antique-style rug lays the right groundwork for a romantic, comfortable room. The pretty, simple bed becomes a lovely focal point when it's pushed against the wall, daybed style, and framed with a graceful swag that suggests a canopy. Designer: Alan Nugent, INTERIORS by Decorating Den.

An array of needlepoint and silky patchwork pillows adds an elegant yet very comfortable feeling to this cozy daybed. With hand-painted murals in every corner, the only wall art needed is the custom name keepsake above the bed.

Red, White, and New

When you want to inject a room with spirit, you can't go wrong with red, white, and blue. Crisp white walls and trim make a great background for a lively, easy-living scheme. This room is cheerful yet comfortably serene—just what you'd want for an active boy. For safety's sake, all furniture corners are rounded, decorations are simple, and there's plenty of room to relax. Accent pillows are an easy way to give the color scheme a big boost, and the fact that they're unbreakable is a nice plus. An armchair and a window bench, both covered in casual denim blue, provide special spots to curl up and read or just hang out. Tortoiseshell bamboo shades are another smart, easy solution that add color and texture without fuss.

A vintage desk has enough room for schoolbooks and small craft projects, but it doesn't take up too much space. A metallic desk lamp provides needed task lighting for study time and provides visual balance to the wood furnishings.

A merry mix of patterns gives this boy's room a high-energy feeling without looking cluttered. A timeless color scheme of red, white, and blue keeps company with the proven boyhood favorites of sailing ships and teddy bears. Designer: Cyndi Tuma. Stylist: Sunday Hendrickson.

A young girl's bath is pretty in pink and white with accents of blue. It ties in nicely with the blue and cream bedroom accented with pink. This balancing of colors is a proven approach to decorating a suite. It relates adjoining rooms without making them too similar.

Sweetness and Light

Traditional charm abounds in this spacious bed-and-bath suite for a young girl. A playful array of patterns gives the room a lively feeling, but that's balanced by large expanses of soothing, pale cream, pink, and blue. Heirloom quilts, a soft rag rug, and pristine vintage linens play a starring role in this frankly sentimental space, but, with the blue and cream backgrounds, it wouldn't be hard to pare down the look for an older girl. For now, romantic touches like the blue sky and bed swathed in tulle and roses provide plenty of atmosphere for modest cost and effort. A setting like this would make any girl feel cherished—what could be sweeter?

A collection of pretty pastel quilts and vintage linens turns this bed into a cuddly, comfortable nest. The garden motif is enhanced by hand-painted floral sprigs on the furniture.

The pastel quilt that hangs behind the bed was the inspiration for this pretty room's color scheme. The simple pencil-post bed is transformed with yards of bridal tulle and silk roses and ivy. Storage built in under the eaves keeps more of the floor clear for play. Designer: Delia Spradley, Spradley Interiors. Sylist: Joetta Moulden.

169

Outlook: Cool and Sunny

Bright and light, hues of blue, green, and yellow are kid-friendly favorites in just about any setting. In these rooms, the appeal of an analogous blue/green/yellow scheme is set off by the warm natural wood tones of the furniture. Pieces with simple, graceful lines and comfortably rounded corners are always winners. The ones shown here are traditionally styled, but it's possible to find "soft contemporary" pieces with a similar pleasing feeling. With colors this inviting, you may want to stick with solids, but stripes, checks, and simple plaids are other popular choices for both boys and girls. If and when your child's tastes change, you can change patterns and colors with ease. The basic furnishings will look just as great, whatever next year's look may be.

Kids everywhere throw clothes, toys, and what have you under the bed anyway, and a captain's bed makes that habit a neat one. Vibrant yellow, green, and blue bedding lends a summery feeling. A coordinating window shade and rug complete the simple scheme. Manufacturer: PJ Kids.

A captain's bed, named for designs used aboard ships, is a great solution for storage in a kid's room. Boys and girls alike will appreciate the good looks of a bed like this, and parents will like the easily accessible storage the lower drawers and cupboards provide. Manufacturer: PJ Kids.

Satiny, naturally finished birch wood and a gently curved traditional design make this inventive group a standout. The unit tucks a full-size computer desk plus drawer and open storage into the base and slides a second bed on casters at right angles to the first. Manufacturer: PJ Kids.

Stylized spaceships decorate these bed linens, but you can find the same richly saturated blue on ocean prints, plaids, and a host of patterns. Or, change the spread to fire engine red and you've got a whole different look without sacrificing the cool, calming power of all-around blue. Stylist: Amy Leonard. Manufacturer: The Glidden Company.

Crayon Box Colors

When your vision for a room is bigger than your budget, reach for a can of paint. It delivers the fastest, biggest change for the smallest investment, and your choices are unlimited. Just changing the wall color will have a great impact, but why stop there? Unite an array of unmatched furniture pieces with paint colors that harmonize with the walls, and you'll have a pulled-together look without breaking the bank. In this room, pale blue walls visually expand the space; rich blue and green furniture blends in and preserves the room's visual flow. Against this cool blue and green background, hot red and yellow accents really pop. What kid wouldn't love it?

A slatted table and chairs create a parklike feeling that's enhanced by the cheerful Kelly green hue. A blackboard framed in the same green turns this corner of the room into a fun study space.

2

Ribbon-Hung Chalkboard

WHAT YOU'LL NEED

Bulletin board
Black chalkboard paint
2 small paintbrushes
6-inch-long piece of trim, same width as frame
Hammer and ¾-inch-long brads or finishing nails
Waterbase latex paint
2 lengths 15-inch grosgrain ribbon, 1 inch wide

1. Paint back side of bulletin board (except frame) with an even coat of black chalkboard paint. Let dry; repeat twice.

2. To make chalk holder, center piece of trim on front of chalkboard over frame. Tack in place with small brads or finishing nails.

3. Paint 2 coats latex paint on chalk holder and frame, letting dry between coats.

4. To attach ribbon, thread end of 1 ribbon length through hanger on back of board, and tie into knot to secure. Repeat for second piece of ribbon. Bring free ends of ribbon together and tie into a knot. Hang on wall as desired.

Garden Flair

The mother of this room's occupant is a Montessori teacher who believes everything around the child will affect the development of her daughter's personality. Inspired by her own childhood garden memories, the mother requested a garden-theme room that could grow along with her young daughter. The decorator obliged with a complementary color scheme and a mix of pretty but not childish fabrics. Walls the color of Granny Smith apples make a background both soothing and lively; accents in rosy red add punch. While the wealth of dressmaker details on pillows and other fabrics are delightful, this room is practical, too. The window seat contains a number of roomy storage drawers, the trundle daybed will host sleepovers through the teen years, and there's plenty of floor space for play.

A curved window seat and matching curved valance make the most of a spectacular window. The sheer curtains can be released to enclose the window seat's private area, which is stocked with pillows and stuffed animals.

A charming mix of sophisticated, cheerful fabrics gives this window seat a feeling that's luxurious yet fun. Adding to the garden ambience, a deep border at baseboard level brings a morning glory–twined picket fence into the room.

A laser-cut border of cascading leaves high on the wall suggests the feeling of an airy pergola. A wrought-iron daybed enhances the airy feeling and is practical for long-term use. Dressmaker details on each of the pillows add extra charm. Designer: Gloria Rinaldi, INTERIORS by Decorating Den.

Lure of the Sea

For a youngster who can't get enough of the water and rustic environs in general, this seafaring space is a permanent island getaway. A small room with awkward eaves may seem an ambitious canvas for a seascape, but a masterpiece of trompe l'oeil painting turns the whole room into a natural setting that blurs the boundaries of ceiling, walls, and floor. Craggy rocks, beach, sea grass, fir trees, rustic little boats, and a sea that meets a cloudy sky all weave a spell. In decorating as in advertising, power comes from having one big idea on which to work variations. With a big idea like the sea, it would be easy to take a side trip from this rustic fishing village to a treasure island or a tropical getaway, depending on your child's personal preference.

A weathered Adirondack chair makes a classic perch for gazing out to sea. A simple desk is inspired by the wood of an old wharf. The hand-painted floorcloth puts sea and sand at a young mariner's feet.

A simple chest with beadboard drawers snuggles under a low eve to provide ample storage in a small space. A flattop seafaring chest works as a toy/storage chest or a casual play table surface.

A simple boat makes a charming bed for a young sailor. Canvas secured with rope repeats the sail motif; a lighthouse bookcase makes the most of a normally wasted corner. Designer: Diane Boyer, ASID, Diane Boyer Interiors, A Division of Bill Behrle Associates. Window treatment: L&G Decorator Workroom. Trompe l'oeil painting: Holsten Interior Artisans.

177

Grade-school Collections

Young grade-schoolers may have a lot in common with their preschool siblings. As yet, they don't need a lot of work space for homework, but they do need a lot of space for play. In a few years, he or she will need a "real" desk and more storage for clothes and personal hobby items. Near the end of this age span, most grade-schoolers have more in common with teens than with little kids, so they'll value privacy and covet work-and-storage space more than ever. At every stage, kids like collections of their own more than knickknacks, but they do enjoy practical accessories that depict their hobbies and interests. A fresh, creative approach really comes in handy here, so figure out what your child's room needs, then scout out items that are fun and functional.

A plantation-style desk and hutch gives a modern computer a charmingly traditional home. Switch the table lamp for a floor lamp and you'd have a work surface for conventional writing, too. Retailer: Bombay Kids.

A clock may be a practical necessity in your grade-schooler's room, but it can be an appealing wall accent, too. With a whimsical clock like the one shown here, even wake-up time can be fairy time. Retailer: Bombay Kids.

When is a shelf not just a shelf? When it's a prop plane that stashes stuff on both tiers of its wings. Whether your child's passion is vehicles, animals, or something else, you'll find cute and practical accessories using favorite motifs. Just a few of these pieces help bring your theme to life. Retailer: Spiegel Catalog, Inc.

Stitched-on or ironed-on appliqués have long been popular on kids' clothes, but they can also give a kicky custom look to ordinary throw pillows. Pick up inexpensive solid-color pillows and add your own designs of cutout fabric, or buy creatively stitched ones like these. Retailer: Bombay Kids.

Flower power comes to the rescue when your child needs a little help keeping track of important papers or when she just wants a casual way to show off memorabilia. Cute and colorful, this little bulletin board is even more fun with mini posy pushpins. Retailer: The Container Store.

Teen Retreats

"Mom, that's so babyish!" These words, so often applied to an outfit or a once-loved toy, can eventually be used to spell the end of a "little kid" bedroom scheme. Even if your youngster's room doesn't have a juvenile theme, he or she may simply be ready for a new look.

Just as adult decorating decisions are often triggered by a life change, such as a new baby or a major social event like an at-home wedding, your child may want to celebrate a personal milestone with a new bedroom. Right before starting

middle school is a popular time to give the bedroom a new personality, but the desire may hit any time between about age nine to sometime in high school. Do your homework and you'll be ready for this adventure whenever it arrives.

With all of today's product choices available in a variety of price ranges, redecorating a room can be a fun project you and your teen or preteen can share. Let your child know you support (within reason) his or her wish for self-expression through room decor and even an independent-minded child will turn to you for help and advice as well as funds.

On the ticklish subject of funds, you may already know that, while kids this age are painfully brand conscious, most have no desire for the high-end looks adults crave. Fun, funky, and free-spirited designs hold more appeal, and even kids who appreciate the finer things are likely to want a more unrestrained version of a traditional look.

If you and your child can come to some agreement about such major items as a desk, a bed, and window treatments, buy the best "real" furnishings your budget allows. Then, fill in with fun, low-cost novelties like beanbag chairs in jellybean colors, funky lamps, and dramatically colored bedding you won't mind replacing when a new look comes along in a few years.

Painted walls are a practical choice at this stage of the game. Paint has a fresh contemporary feeling, and, better yet, it's the least expensive, fastest way to make a big change in a room. You'll want to tell your child that paint looks a lot darker and more vivid on four walls than in a tiny paint chip and that professional designers usually advocate choosing a color two or three steps lighter than the color you like best on the paint chip. That said, buy the smallest container you can of several colors in the running, and have your child paint an area about three feet square on one wall with each of the colors. Let your child choose the hue that looks best. (One big exception to starting with the paint color is if your child has already picked out a fabric. Then, you'll probably want to suggest paint to coordinate with the lightest color in the fabric.)

Youngsters are trying on nothing less than their own self definitions when they embark on a room redecoration, so be patient. You can be a big help in minimizing impulsive decisions your child may regret without making your intervention into a power struggle. Try playing interior decorator with your child as the client: When a few choices have been identified, tape fabric and paint swatches and photos of selected window treatments, accessories, etc., on a large piece of white poster board. Your child will be able to see at a glance what

works and what doesn't. If you find it too confusing to pull all their likes together in a visually coherent way, keep in mind that, in general, preteens and teens want either a very dramatic room or one that looks as much like a studio apartment as possible.

If you have any extra money or ingenuity to spend on this project, use it to create as much storage as possible. Include both open/display and hidden, and, above all, make storage easily accessible if you want them to use it. This is one area in which little kids and big ones are pretty similar!

If your teen is older, you may want to consider how you'll use the room once he or she is independent. If the room will become a home office, a daybed may be the best choice. If it will become a full-time guest room, you can go with a full- or queen-size bed with all the trimmings. Either way, your grownup child's old room will still say "welcome home." What could be better?

Color Me Confident

Fearless, passionate color electrifies these teen rooms with individuality and youthful flair. The eye appeal of the spaces illustrates an established decorating rule: You can use a variety of strong colors in one room if they're of a similar intensity that creates balance. Color is the most compelling, emotionally charged element in any decorating scheme, and, for many youngsters, identifying a favorite color is important to developing a sense of self. These cheerful rooms show how far you can go to indulge a favorite hue or two—and still have a room you won't need to close the door on. So go ahead and indulge your child in his or her best-loved shades. Simple treatments and a few well-placed neutrals can tame the mix in style.

Dramatic fuchsia, magenta, and shocking pink fill this room with luscious color that feels like waking up in the heart of a flower. A Mondrian-inspired graphic on the wall echoes the rich colors and geometric shapes of the silk pillows. Shots of black and white keep the look from becoming too sweet. Retailer: Bombay Kids.

Chartreuse, royal blue, purple, and scarlet make an edgy scheme that's great for a confident, creative youngster. The mix of modern and traditional furniture gets even more zip with shots of black and white. A look this funky can be created with repainted and recovered hand-me-downs and resale shop finds.

Animal prints are wildly appealing when paired with gilt, scrolls, and flirty fringe. Star treatment like this can turn even a lamp from a resale shop into a retro fashion accent. When a room is filled with intense color, rely on black and white to add cool drama and visual relief. Retailer: Bombay Kids.

Vibrant violet makes a great background for a room that's dramatic, airy, and very hip. Low-cost Japanese paper globe lanterns, sari-inspired silks, and simple white furniture are charming and lighthearted—just like the room's young occupant. Retailer: Bombay Kids.

Tropical Getaway

Nature offers endless inspiration for decorating schemes that appeal to both sexes and all ages. These rooms celebrate tropical plants and animals in a variety of ways, from botanical fish pillows to marine life prints. In one setting, the bed is given focal-point importance with the use of a simple mosquito-netting canopy crown. In the other, a bed tucked into a window alcove and piled with pillows has the look of a daybed/studio couch. In both rooms, print fabrics establish the tropical, youthful mood. Green, blue, sand, and white are naturals for an ocean theme, but coral, shrimp pink, and other hues also swim into view. Perfect for a warm climate, these tropical looks may be even more appealing in a cold-weather setting or an urban environment.

Designed around a theme of tropical marine life, this versatile room is set up as a studio apartment. A bedspread with whimsical turtles takes center stage, but the sisal rug and fern-print shades and pillows depicting tropical fish all add to the breezy look. A Chinese fish kite makes a clever wall accent. Designer: Janet Lohman Interior Design.

A colorful underwater scene pairs with an ocean-blue-and-white print for a look that's pretty but not too sweet. A nondescript window gains importance with full-length curtains hung at ceiling height. The bed's funky hula skirt and mosquito netting canopy add a touch of fantasy and fun. Designer: Janet Lohman Interior Design.

Playful Color

The right colors can do a lot for your outlook, and your teen is at least as sensitive to emotional currents as you are. You can't protect her from every bump, but, when she gets home, you can wrap her in a comforting, uplifting environment that starts with colors she loves. Once you've nailed the color scheme, furniture and accessories can be much easier to pull together. If you're shopping, a new bedroom group in warm wood looks great against cool-colored walls, while warm-tinted walls take the chill out of cool laminates. Choose a contrasting color or two for accents; when the mood strikes, she can change them and get a whole new look with the basic background hue. That's a guaranteed mood-lifter.

Rich turquoise and white make a cool, pretty background for notes of fresh yellow and hot pink. A variety of easily removable translucent hooks, clips, and mounts lets her change her decorating accents with ease. Mounting devices: 3M.

A high-ceilinged room looks even more spacious swathed in pale sky blue, but this tint creates an expansive feeling no matter what the actual room size. A deeper shade of turquoise adds depth; contrasting bright orange and lighthearted lime green inject pure excitement. Manufacturer: Stanley Furniture Co.

Apricot and coral swaddle this room in sherbet colors. Happy tints are an easy way to soften the utilitarian angles of Eurostyle modern furniture without sacrificing the sleek minimalist look.

Storybook Cottage

A romantic-hearted girl of any age would fall in love with this utterly charming room. Decorated in English country style, the room wraps its occupant in warm and gentle garden hues. It's a timeless look, but one easygoing enough for a young girl who'd like to feel more grown up. Washable fabrics and a mix of casual rattan and repainted old furniture give this room a touchable, "unprissy" comfort today's girls expect, without sacrificing a bit of romance. Well-thought-out storage all around the room, from a display shelf above the window to a rustic china hutch, offers plenty of ways to tame clutter. Vintage-style quilts, pillows, and other bed linens are hot right now so their gentle charm is as easy to find as it is to live with.

A comfy cushioned window seat piled with pillows makes an inviting spot for reading, daydreaming, or quiet play. A modified crown canopy adds a little extra aura of romance. Vintage and casual rattan furniture give a warm heirloom feeling to the room. Designer: Debra Jones, Ray Kinner Builders.

A delightfully old-fashioned dressing table with a triptych mirror lends fairy tale appeal to an already charming setting. A slipper chair is always romantic, but, covered in washable white cotton, it's also kid-friendly.

A graceful camelback loveseat in white is perfectly at home in a youngster's room thanks to a casual washable slipcover. White beadboard paneling halfway up the wall adds to the airy look; its painted surface is easy to care for.

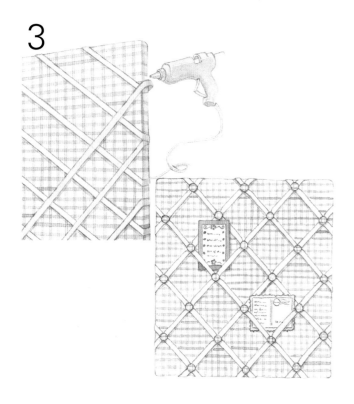

Easy Chic

If you think you have to invest in a wealth of brand-new matching furniture to set up a cool teen's room, take a second look. Pink and white never looked so hip! A collection of unmatched pieces with graceful lines finds a home in these rather spacious rooms, but, even without the square footage, a space like this is anything but square. Are these pieces French antiques or just inspired finds? Who needs to know? The classic girl's room recipe of powder pink and white is enlivened by touches of dramatic black plus a rainbow of interesting jewel tones. Look for furniture like this everywhere from casual outdoor furniture stores to resale shops, and keep function in mind. Without trying too hard, the result is an enviable offhand charm that can go the distance.

Ribbon Bulletin Board

WHAT YOU'LL NEED
2 pieces of cork, each 16 inches square
16-inch square foam core
Craft glue
20-inch square quilt batting, ½ inch thick
20-inch square cotton fabric
Hot-temperature glue gun and glue sticks
6 yards satin or grosgrain ribbon, ½ inch wide
Scissors
Tape measure
15 to 18 matching buttons
Matching thread and needle

1. Use craft glue to attach cork piece to foam, and let dry. Glue second cork piece on top of first; let dry.

2. Place batting over board so 2 inches hangs over on each side. Hot glue batting edges to back of board, making sure it is straight and lies smooth. Put fabric over batting, and secure in same manner as batting.

3. Starting in bottom left corner, stretch piece of ribbon diagonally over board. Let last 2 inches of each ribbon wrap around back of board. Glue ends in place. Continue attaching ribbon, moving up board diagonally and spacing each ribbon 4 inches apart. When completed diagonally in 1 direction, attach ribbon in opposite diagonal direction to create a checkerboard effect.

4. Position button over intersection of 2 ribbons, and stitch in place. Repeat at all ribbon intersections.

A black garden bench has an airy look that keeps it in sync with the light look of this room. A pair of full-length curtains in an artful plaid makes a colorful room divider. Wicker baskets and a quartet of message boards stash stuff in an organized way. Designer: Laura Bohn Design Associates. Architect: Shope Reno Wharton.

Skip those skimpy nightstands: A graceful round table offers plenty of room for a lamp, books, and more. A French-style bed with a chic leather-upholstered headboard injects the touch of black often recommended by interior designers.

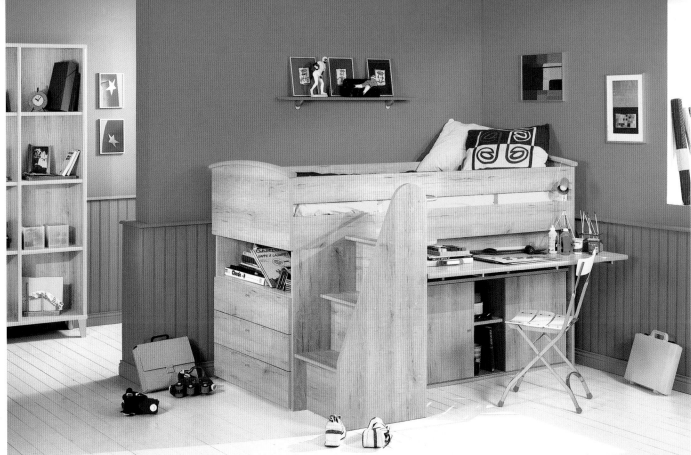

A bunk bed for one makes excellent use of the area under the bed with an array of savvy storage sections. A comfortable staircase and built-in desk with a roomy work surface are all part of the kid-friendly package. Retailer: Gautier USA, Inc.

Naturally Smart

If you and your child appreciate modern style, you may be open to today's inventive combination units that put sleep, storage, study, and play areas all together. Cleverly designed and wonderfully functional, these spacesaving systems have warm appeal when they're made of naturally finished wood. When it comes to decorating a room around a unit like this, soft contemporary style is a natural. Bright colors and stylized motifs lend a cheerful note that appeals to any age, from tot to teen. To complete the room, desks, bookcases, and other furniture pieces are widely available in naturally finished wood. Look for those with polyurethane-lacquered worktops that extend the life of the wood without obscuring its attractive grain. Can you have a casual room and substantial furniture? Naturally!

When two kids share a room, bunk beds are a popular way to keep the peace and make the best use of space. This inventive design features a real staircase that is much safer than the usual bunk bed ladder and offers informal cubbyholes for storage, too. Retailer: Gautier USA, Inc.

This girl's room is in a modern house with traditional furniture, so an eclectic approach isn't out of the ordinary for this family. The white walls and antiques could be a bit austere, but that's no problem here. Colorful, whimsical artworks and coordinating fabrics give this space a delightful young feeling that's fresh as spring yet timeless.

Happy Individualist

Teens love the latest anything, and they want their rooms to reflect their forward-looking perspective. How that actually plays out, however, will be a function of your own approach. If you love modern style in all its incarnations, an unabashedly "today" space for your teen will fit right in. If you don't already have the furnishings on hand, pick up funky fashion-forward pieces wherever you can find them. If you prefer investment furnishings, you can give your teen a hip young slant on the classics with a few modern approaches. Gallery white or boldly colored walls and furniture with simple bold lines create a no-fuss feeling. Add contemporary art and colorful geometric-pattern fabrics to carry out the theme with flair.

Pink and black is a frisky '50s scheme that's now more fun than ever. This wild room starts with a totally edgy bed that combines metal grids and laced faux pony skin, but it shows a sweet side with powder pink accents, some vintage, some utterly 21st century. Stylist: Sunday Hendrickson.

Soft Impressions

If you prefer to invest in traditionally styled furniture but your teen longs for a more modern look, one easy way to compromise is with fabrics and colors. This room's scheme of pale lime and lilac creates an airy, youthful feeling that's enhanced by the contemporary floral patterns. Adding to the lighthearted ambience, trompe l'oeil lattice and vines are hand-painted on the wall. You could create a similar effect with just about any other fresh, light color scheme, such as aqua and peach. To create a modern feeling with traditional furniture, keep the backgrounds simple—no busy wallpapers or elaborate draperies. Contemporary prints, such as these abstract watercolor florals (large scale for the bed, smaller scale for the window valance), enhance the fun-loving look.

Traditional dark mahogany furniture stands out dramatically against pale lilac walls. The lightly scaled writing desk takes to occasional computer use with ease. White moire roller blinds trimmed in mauve gimp add a subtly pretty layer under floral valances.

A wrought-iron bed with organic leaf, bud, and vine motifs is a lovely centerpiece for a garden-inspired boudoir. Silk flowering vines enhance the color scheme and take the look to a new level.

Contemporary floral and plaid prints in soft lime, lilac, and white create a romantic scheme she won't outgrow. Silk flowering vines entwined around a wrought-iron bed canopy make a chic flower bower. Designer: Susan Comfort, INTERIORS by Decorating Den.

This lucky young man's bedroom sports a real (albeit scaled-down) basketball court done up in his favorite team's colors. The cabinet hides home electronics; the unique headboard shelving echoes the Cubist-inspired bed ensemble. Designer: Montanna & Associates. Architect: Tom Price.

Sports trophies, musical keyboards, limited-edition cartoon art, and other evidence of well-rounded interests abound in this teen's room, but the effect is sleek and uncluttered. Eurostyle laminates in gunmetal gray wrap the room in unobtrusive high performance.

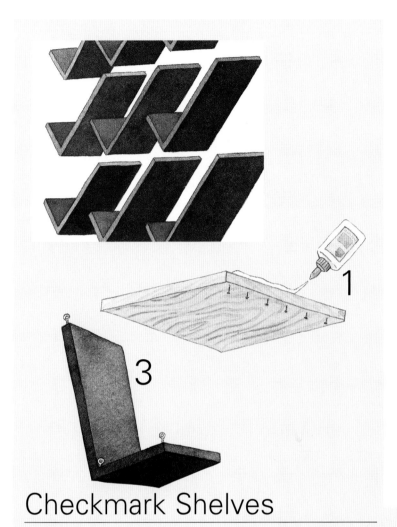

Sport Authorities

Successful, active teens have more complicated studies and more elaborate hobbies than their younger siblings, but they're still kids who need room to move. Sleek, well-designed storage furniture can house a multitude of things in an orderly way. Even if orderliness is too much to hope for, furnishings like these at least keep the clutter out of sight and off the floor. If your teen appreciates the natural warmth of wood furniture and built-ins, follow through with fabrics that echo these tawny tones. If he prefers an industrial look, you can furnish his space with laminates in cool neutral shades and inject a bit of warmth with red or another hot accent color. Either way, strive for simplicity, minimal hardware, and maximum freedom of movement.

Checkmark Shelves

WHAT YOU'LL NEED (FOR EACH CHECKMARK)
2 lengths 1×10-inch pine shelving, 10 and 20 inches long
Hammer and 4 to 6 brads
Wood glue
Damp rag
Fine-grade sandpaper
Paint and paintbrush
Pencil
Screws and ¾-inch-wide keyhole plates, 3 each
3 drywall anchors
Screwdriver

1. Using hammer, tap brads about 1½ inches apart along 1 side edge of 10-inch length of shelving so brads are secure but not through wood. Apply line of glue along same edge on opposite side of brads.

2. Place 20-inch length of shelving perpendicular to other piece so edges are aligned. Hammer pieces together; wipe away excess glue. Let dry, then sand smooth and wipe clean. Apply 2 coats of paint; let dry between coats.

3. Position shelving on wall as desired, marking screw holes with pencil. Attach keyhole plates to edge of checkmark at top, bottom, and top of bottom portion of checkmark. Using screwdriver and drywall anchors, secure screws into wall, leaving unscrewed about ¼ inch. Hang shelf onto screws.

4. Repeat steps for more checkmark shelves.

Definitely Hot

Once upon a time, you weren't supposed to use hot pink and orange together, but the '60s changed all that. Today's teens love the intensity of these saturated tropical color combinations. As exciting as they are, hot colors can be wonderfully livable. Just balance areas of dazzling color with areas of white, another neutral, or a pale tint of one of your hot colors. Funky flowers are a great motif for this color scheme, but just about any motif your teen enjoys can be worked into a one-of-a-kind design. Florals are just the start of what you can find in today's contemporary fabrics, wallcoverings, and accessories, so let your girl shop for her current favorites. Balance busy prints with areas of solid color to create visual breathing room.

Patchwork gets a hip new look in a contemporary watercolor print of sunny yellow and deep pinks. Some bed ensembles are available with window treatments and other accessories, but you can achieve a similar look just by sticking to a scheme of two or three key colors. Retailer: JCPMedia L.P.

The joys of shopping, phoning, and primping parade across a frisky print wall border and coordinating sheets. If she tires of the pattern, it's simple to replace it with another print or solid. Lime, perhaps? Retailer: JCPMedia L.P.

Bunk beds for big girls are perfect for sleepovers and save floor space for more fun pursuits. Large areas of brilliant sunset orange are balanced by lots of cooling white and naturally finished wood floors. Manufacturer: Stanley Furniture Co.

Space-Age Sleek

Just how modern can contemporary style be? Very! Teens are essentially forward-looking beings, so it's no surprise they're often attracted to sleek modern style. There's a practical aspect, too: If your teen's room is small, simply styled light-color modern furniture can help it look more spacious, and laminate surfaces make cleaning a breeze. What's more, even lightly scaled modern pieces may be big on savvy storage. Decorating's a snap as well. You can emphasize the cool spacious factor with blue and green backgrounds and add warmth with yellow and orange. Furniture like this would be as much at home in a first studio apartment as in a teen's bedroom, so, if you shop carefully for quality, you might be able to send him or her off with the basics.

Everything an active young student might need is close at hand in this cleverly designed room. Several different types of work areas, a bed with an extra trundle below, and storage units that handle everything from cassettes to full-length coats are all part of the Eurostyle package. Retailer: Gautier USA, Inc.

If your teen has the room, you can go beyond bedroom basics and add pieces that befit a chic studio apartment. A generously scaled wall unit offers extra display and storage space, a coffee table adds comfort to any seating area, and a lightly scaled dining/work table is hardworking and versatile. Retailer: Gautier USA, Inc.

Blue Reigns

Not every girl goes for pink in a big way, and some lose interest in it when they reach their teens. No problem! Versatile and popular, blue is just as likely to win her favor. Blue is widely used in the bedroom because it's inherently soothing. In a south- or west-facing bedroom, the color is a practical choice because it's psychologically cooling. What's more, if your teen's room is on the small side, pale tints of blue work like white to visually expand the space. Virtually any color looks fine with some tone of blue, but you may want to create contrast with darks and lights. Royal or navy blue comes alive with yellow; pale blue looks sophisticated next to deep magenta or fuchsia. Either way, blue is clearly cool.

If your girl has a decorative wrought-iron bed, it can be fun to pick out some of the motifs with contrasting enamel paint. The sunflower motif on this bed is repeated in a cheerful wallpaper border; painting the area above the border enhances the room's distinctive look.

Creamy yellow glazes simple furniture for a luscious look that's rich against French blue walls. Sophisticated prints on the bed and a funky modern lamp give this room grown-up cachet. Manufacturer: EG Furniture.

Polka dots and perky retro-inspired prints in vivid shades of fuchsia and other bold hues give a pale blue-and-white room pizzazz. Manufacturer: The Warm Biscuit Bedding Co.

Rustic Retreats

Teens crave a space of their own to get away from it all, and these handsome rooms fulfill that need without any fuss. Whether the room is as small as a bunkhouse or as big as all outdoors, the style known as "lodge" can make it a getaway any boy would enjoy. Start with simple squared-off furniture in strongly grained oak or pine, or go for even more rustic pieces made of coarse-hewn or peeled logs. Add homespun fabrics in ticking stripes, lumberjack plaid, or other timeless country patterns. A color scheme of red and hunter green or red and denim blue will give a rich, lively contrast to neutral wood tones. Let your boy's interests dictate the accessories, whether he's into cowboys or camping.

Weathered red, white, blue, and forest green are classic lodge colors you can mix and match with ease. Look for ticking stripes, flannel checks, and just about any plaid for a cozy homespun feeling. Retailer: The Magic Moon.

Bunk beds are good, but bunk beds crafted from gnarled natural logs are great. Wood is finished with polyurethane for a smooth snag-free surface and increased durability. A novelty "rodeo" rug and a countrified braided rag rug define areas of the room. Retailer: The Magic Moon.

A big room can still be cozy with a warm color scheme like this one. Forest green and taupe bring the calm tones of nature indoors; bright cardinal scarlet adds punch. A captain's bed with under-the-bed storage drawers help keep things neat. Manufacturer: Stanley Furniture Co.

Fresh and Frolicsome

Yellow-green the color of young lettuce is one of the most versatile hues around. Virtually every color pairs nicely with it, from sedate navy to cheery orange. But, when you pair yellow-green with red-violet, its color wheel complement, you get a scheme that's truly delightful. This room shows how foolproof it can be. Against a chartreuse ground, bright white and magenta stand out as freshly as tulips in a spring field. Even if your furniture is a darker wood you don't want to paint, this green keeps the whole scheme light and bright. It's a look that's fun and feminine and not at all babyish. If your girl is looking for a more sophisticated take on pastel pink and green, this may be it!

To stash home entertainment equipment, a computer desk, or just the usual array of childhood collections, you can't beat a pretty armoire like this one. Louvered doors and a crisp white finish give a feeling of tropical island freshness.

When she's too busy to bother with hangers in the closet, this pretty and practical little mirror helps out with convenient clothing hooks. A coat tree or cheval mirror are charming alternatives. White-painted accessories are easy to find, but just about any workable piece can be painted to coordinate with the room.

When you've got a garden-fresh color scheme like this, there's no need for anything as obvious as floral prints. Instead, a bed ensemble of frisky butterflies gives a fresh twist on springtime style. A rich plaid adds a chic tailored touch. Retailer: Bombay Kids.

Elaborate rococo lamps might look too formal for a teen's room but not when they're topped with lusciously colored silk shades and trimmed in flirty beads, baubles, and fringe. Trims like these let you introduce additional colors or repeat a key tint that helps tie the room together.

Cool and Clear

Blue and white is a timeless scheme that appeals equally to boys and girls, big kids and small. In a stressful world, blue can bring home a serene feeling—something a teen may especially appreciate. If your youngster's room is on the small side, a blue-and-white scheme creates a more spacious feeling, too. To start the decorating process, let your child choose a shade of blue he or she likes best. Sky blue and baby blue are lighthearted favorites that work well in a contemporary setting. For a traditional scheme, rich cobalt is the classic most associated with blue-and-white porcelain. Don't stop there, however. There are many other blues from which to choose, from teal and turquoise to periwinkle and indigo. Whatever shade appeals to your teen, blue really goes the distance.

Pale blue and white look great with modern furniture, especially when you use accents in vibrant red. Extending the contemporary feeling, a traditional wood floor gets a totally updated look with a playful design of blue and white. Retailer: Gautier USA, Inc.

Light and medium blue tones plus white appeal to boys and girls alike. This boy's room stays shipshape (well, almost) thanks to a captain's bed with a lower storage drawer. A wood floor painted white works well with shiny chrome accents. Retailer: Gautier USA, Inc.

A Personal Passion

Teens are great candidates for fearless decorating schemes: Where else can they be this expressive—even rebellious—without the side effects? If you've got a live wire in your household, a campy scheme may be just what they had in mind. Even better from a parent's point of view, a close look at this room shows reassuringly conventional "bones." The Shaker-style bed, traditional end table, animal-print bedding, and neutral-color floor could work in any setting and outlast any fad. The wild look of this room is achieved almost completely with inexpensive paint and a handful of kitschy accessories. A high-spirited trio of tones—aqua, magenta, and purple—gives this room its youthful energy, but any high-contrast cheerful scheme would work. The result? Dramatic, exuberant, and loads of fun—just like your favorite teen.

Hunk-a-burning love: A fireplace, closed off and painted magenta pink, makes a funky shrine to the King. A wall niche, a shallow closet, or another architectural element could be used in similar fashion to showcase favorite treasures or current rock star souvenirs.

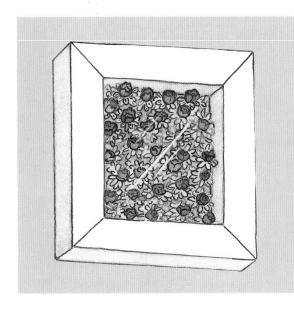

Garden Patch Wallhanging

In this room, the homeowners hung a mat of silk flowers on the wall. To refine the look, frame the mat of flowers. First remove back and glass from shadow frame, then position frame over mat. Trim mat to fit inside frame. Reattach back to frame.

To frame loose flowers, position frame over floral foam, and trim foam to fit inside frame. Cut stems to 1¼ inches. Dip stem into craft glue, then poke into floral foam. Continue gluing flowers to foam to create a dense flower mat.

Leopard prints are a versatile addition to many decorating schemes, but against these hot colors, they're really a walk on the wild side. Botticelli's classic Venus keeps company with Elvis in this campy scheme.

Timely Teen Things

By the time your child is a teen, you may be more interested in updating his or her room than starting from scratch. If your teen's bed and storage units are still looking good and working well, hang onto those college funds. Just freshen the room with new wall paint, stylish new sheets, and some special accent pieces. Your teen's favorite colors and interests make a great launching point, but don't be afraid to indulge in a few frankly fun fad ideas (with your teen's approval, of course). To create more storage for your busy teen, look for clever little solutions instead of big space-hogging ones. If you're looking to make one investment purchase, make it a great state-of-the-art desk and an ergonomic chair.

Graphic designs on CD covers make a dramatic statement, so why not make the most of them to decorate your teen's room? This sleek black tri-panel screen shows off CDs as artwork, keeps them easily accessible, and works as a unique room divider—all at the same time. Retailer: Spiegel.

Modern style takes a fun-loving turn with a lamp that gives new meaning to "lighthearted." A trio of translucent shades in bright primary colors adds a rich glow to cool metal fixtures with a whimsical twist. Task lighting never looked so amusing. Retailer: JCPMedia L.P.

Beanbag chairs have been a kid's-room favorite since the '60s, and for good reason: They're portable, affordable, comfortable, and fun. Plus, they stand up to all the lounging and rollicking around teens can deliver. In chic neutral colors, they'll really go the distance. Retailer: JCPMedia L.P.

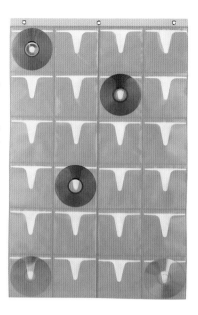

CDs deserve a safe home, but a teen's room may not have the space for stacking jewel cases or special CD-tower furniture. This simple storage unit hangs flat, out of the way, and makes it easy to access up to 24 CDs. Retailer: The Container Store.

Slang words come and go, but teens want to be up-to-the-moment with them. Slogan-sparked toss pillows let you indulge in the latest without a big commitment from your furnishings budget. They're the perfect way to punch up a color scheme, too. Retailer: JCPMedia L.P.

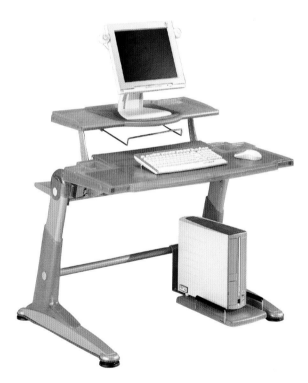

If your young man has more caps than all the New York Yankees put together, they don't need to get scattered and squashed all over his closet. This clever space-saving cap rack stacks 'em up neatly, within easy reach. Retailer: The Container Store.

If you've got a teen who virtually lives in tomorrowland, indulge his modern tastes with a state-of-the-art desk. Sleek as a spaceship, this desk is a springboard for flights of fancy and a workhorse for down-to-earth homework. Retailer: Gautier USA, Inc.

Other Kid-Friendly Spaces

Not too long ago, rooms set aside specifically as playrooms and bathrooms for children were a special luxury. Now, they're simply special. As most parents and teachers can tell you, any room is a potential playroom from a kids'-eye view. Still, there are important differences between recreational rooms and bathrooms kids use along with adults and those specifically designed for kids. Many have to do with safety; others with function. Happily, some also have to do with fun!

PLAYROOMS: LIVABLE AND PRACTICAL

There are several strong reasons to carve out a playroom in your home, and they have to do with the nature of kids. If you live in a climate that allows comfortable outdoor play year-round, a dedicated playroom may not be necessary. Many of us, however, endure long months of cold, and it's a challenge to give kids the opportunities they crave for active play on a daily basis. Here's where a "real" playroom can make a real difference. If you don't want to live with everything laminate for 20 years or have your nice furnishings at risk all the time, a playroom can really help keep the peace.

Where to find space? Even if it's in the basement, today's playroom differs from the old 1950s recreation room in that it's much brighter and lighter. If a basement is your best bet, paint that old brown wood paneling a

warm white, and put down a vinyl or porcelain tile floor. Install ample ceiling light fixtures for the size of your room (don't skimp) and use the latest advances in bulbs that mimic natural daylight. To get the benefit of real sunlight, a room over the garage is a smart alternative, as is the "bonus room" found in many of today's big new houses.

Wherever you locate the playroom, you'll want lighting that's protected from the occasional football toss; easy-care flooring; and comfortable, movable, easy-to-clean furnishings. Plan different zones with wipe-clean flooring for messy play

and softer floor coverings for active play and lounging around. Beanbag chairs and sectionals with washable slipcovers increase the comfort level; indulge in cheerful colors kids love. A workstation or desk with an ergonomic chair can extend the playroom's use for homework, but, even if you only need play surfaces, make sure all corners and edges are rounded for safety.

KIDS' BATHS: SAFETY AND STYLE

Baths used by adults (either parents or guests) and children require some finessing. If this is your situation, the best decorating approach may be grownup but casual. Fussy draperies and delicate, glamorous accessories would be out of place here, but timeless materials and casually elegant touches can please adults and survive the kids, too. A washable poly/rayon shower curtain with the look of raw silk; granite, marble, or ceramic tiles; and washable walls painted with a faux finish design would do the job nicely.

If you're designing a bath for use just by kids, you can take a friskier path. You may want to keep costly installed materials fairly neutral, but you can go wild with everything else. Brightly painted walls make a huge impact, and, even better, they're easy and inexpensive to change; the same goes for towels and nonslip bath rugs. Colorful toothbrush holders and other practical accessories can really enhance your theme, whether it's Barbie or the Great Barrier Reef. For an amusing one-of-a-kind touch, replace ordinary vanity door and drawer pulls with ceramic ones that match your color scheme. If the bath is one several kids will share, try to provide some privacy, whether it's a semienclosed toilet alcove or simply an opaque shower curtain. Separate storage is important in any bath, even if it's just one drawer or a basket under the sink.

Whether your kids' bath is shared or not, safety will be your primary concern. Just for kids, you'll want a sturdy, low step stool for little ones to reach the sink and rest their feet

while using the toilet. You'll also want to use shatterproof acrylic or plastic accessories, such as toothbrush holders and drinking cups. Most other safety features, however, are just as appropriate for baths used by adults or big kids. Rounded corners and edges, nonslip backings on rugs, and grab bars in the shower or bath (screwed into a wall stud, not just hung on like a towel bar) are important. Antiscald devices to prevent hot water burns are essential.

Today's families appreciate the value of universal design ideas like these that make a small-fry spa just as useful when Grandma arrives for the weekend. When it comes to the bathroom, safety is always in style.

Tropical Treat

You may live in a chilly northern city, but there's no reason your little one can't dwell in a tropical paradise. To create the look, skip the temperamental orchids, and reach for economical easy-care paint. This room starts with a brilliant sunshine yellow base then adds rainbow hues. Lightweight plastic furniture is drenched in color and molded to be smooth and free of sharp corners. Other accessory pieces are painted in the same happy-go-lucky hues. In a situation like this, it pays to be bold: The ho-hum fireplace, for example, gets a whole new life with a coat of hot pink paint. Handsome wood flooring is finished in its natural color; a pale neutral does a nice job of grounding the look.

If your child's playroom includes less-than-exciting features like this fireplace, don't try to make it into something it's not. If it is too prominent to "disappear" by painting it the same as the walls, do this instead: Treat the item as a piece of sculpture and paint it an unexpected color.

Whether you choose lightweight molded plastic furniture or warm wood furniture painted colorfully, be certain it's safe for little ones. Choose pieces that are sturdy (kids stand as well as sit on chairs, no matter what we say), make sure that plastic edges don't have rough burrs and that wood edges are sanded smooth.

Bright and Bouncy

Colorfully patterned alphabet letters dance along a cheerful shower curtain designed with kids in mind. With white walls, floor, and fixtures, any color scheme would pop; when the choice is bright happy colors like these, the room is as much fun as a circus. Retailer: Garnet Hill.

If you've got a child's bath you just don't know what to do with, give everything a clean coat of white. Then, spark it up with your child's favorite colors or, simpler yet, an array of bright primary and secondary colors. They're fun and reassuring for kids of all ages. Then, carry out the simple energizing look with an array of easy-to-love motifs. This room uses polka dots, green grass, and a few other easily identifiable designs. You might prefer stylized blossoms, stars, rainbows, or other elements that appeal to your child. Throw in a few alphabet letters or numerals in a range of colors. Spell out your child's name and you've got a proven winner.

Decorate an old-fashioned white claw-foot bathtub with giant polka dots? Why not? Attach self-adhesive nonskid dots to the bottom to help prevent slips, and, for fun, extend some of the dots up onto the walls of the tub.

A fun retro-style cabinet makes a smart little medicine chest. Be sure yours has a safety latch if younger children will use the bath. To keep it out of kids' way, have the chest mounted above chair-rail height as it is here.

Are these whimsical toothbrush towel hooks really toothbrushes or just pretend? Who cares? These days, it's easy to convert nontraditional items into useful hooks or pegs and even easier to find witty accessories that look just like daisies, sailboats, or whatever. Check sophisticated children's catalogs and on-line retailers.

Urban Fairyland

While most wall murals in children's rooms depict the long ago and faraway lands of fairy tales, some go for a different geography. For a lucky child living in an urban setting, this room celebrates the here and now with a wonderful view of a city park in springtime. This winsome mural visually expands the already spacious room and creates the effect of walking into a cheerful, contemporary children's book. It also reminds adults and kids alike that magical locales are all around us. If there's a special place your child loves, or if you'd just like to show the place you live in its most romantic light, a mural like this would be a great start.

A wonderful mural wraps this room in everyday magic. Rendered in lighthearted pastels, even the office buildings take on a hopeful glow. Surrounding park lands depict a zoo, fountains, and other "real life" elements, seen through a child's perspective. The floor pattern is actually a whimsical version of a dollhouse floorplan.

A beautiful bay window would be a treasure anywhere, but a roomy cushioned window seat makes it fun and inviting in this lucky girl's room. You could seat a whole Brownie troop on this one! Designer: Kathryne Dahlman, Kathryne Designs.

Wild About Art

Fearless, vigorous, and intensely colorful: Artwork bursting with passionate energy covers most of the surfaces in this one-of-a-kind playroom. The teenage musician who hangs out in this lively space can practice his instruments or entertain his pals without disturbing the family. Cushy sofas in cool spill-hiding black get extra punch from neon-bright toss pillows and lacquered furniture in primary hues. A collection of tray tables covered in edgy modern designs provides lots of extra flexible surfaces for snacking or small projects, and an easy-care hard-surface floor is treated to wildly colorful squiggles on black. To keep things from getting visually out of hand, large wall areas are left serenely white. Exciting and practical, this space earns its keep by keeping up with all the demands a literal "playroom" makes.

Artwork Aplenty

Tabletops, floors, walls, doors—virtually any surface in your home can become a canvas for your budding artists. Before your junior Picasso wields his or her brush, here are some prepwork pointers for a variety of surfaces.

Walls—Fill a mop bucket with all-purpose dish detergent diluted with warm water. Using a sponge, gently wash wall with solution, removing smudges, dirt, and grime. This will help paint adhere to surface. Paint as desired.

Wood tabletops and floors—If painting only a section of floor or table, use painter's tape to outline area. Using fine-grade sandpaper, sand area lightly to remove wax or varnish build-up, but not so deep as to remove all layers of finish (keeping lower layers of finish intact protects wood and keeps paint from seeping into grain). Wipe area clean with a damp cloth, then with a dry cloth to remove all dust. Paint as desired; when dry, seal with a clear matte varnish.

Plastic–Lightly scuff surface with sandpaper so paint will stick to plastic. Wipe clean with a damp cloth. Paint as desired, then seal with a light coat of clear varnish spray.

Concrete–Scrub surface with all-purpose dish detergent diluted with warm water. When dry, paint with 2 coats of clear varnish to seal, allowing varnish to dry between coats. Paint as desired, then seal with another coat of clear varnish.

Linoleum–Scrub surface with all-purpose dish detergent diluted with warm water. When dry, paint as desired, then seal with a coat of clear varnish.

A quartet of unique paintings gives versatile collapsible tray tables fabulous presence that lights up the whole room, whether they're in use or just displayed out of the way. A white-painted brick wall invites another abstract painting. Commission a professional or enlist your favorite student artist to create your own unique look.

Even without the artwork-embellished tray tables, this room enjoys lots of visual pizzazz. Starting with eminently practical black sofas and floor, these owners injected a lively spirit with colorful squiggles, dots, and stripes.

Rustic with a Twist

Rustic style can mean anything from camping and Old West themes to modern looks with a few interesting rough edges. These two kids' bathrooms illustrate the breadth of rustic style with children in mind. In a bedroom/bath suite, it's once upon a time in the West thanks to an array of cowboy images, fabrics, and accents. The other bath is a breezy ocean-inspired room with a casual contemporary flair. Both rooms rely on lots of fresh white and generous areas of naturally finished wood for backgrounds. This white-plus-wood combo is a calm, timeless winner that can go a variety of ways depending on your theme accents. These rooms use soft blue, bright red, and a bit of yellow as accent colors. The finished effects are quite different, but both are proven kid-pleasers.

Bright and breezy yet warm and natural, this shipshape kids' bath celebrates beachfront living with easygoing flair. A few fun, colorful accents, including a hand-painted mirror and ceramic accessories, add excitement to a calm background.

A fire engine red clawfoot bathtub deserves the dramatic treatment it gets from a handsome curtained alcove. Red bandannas make the perfect little window valance and curtain tiebacks.

A serious home studio for young artists includes easy-care surfaces, ample storage with funky door pulls, and even a giant chalkboard created right on the wall with special paint. Designer: Carol Spong, ASID; Carol Spong, ASID Interior Design.

Nurturing Young Talents

Computers are certainly here to stay, and they'll be even more prominent in kids' lives tomorrow than they are today. That doesn't mean you shouldn't encourage your kids in more creative low-tech hobbies and pursuits, however. Children of all ages enjoy drawing, coloring, painting, taking photographs, and, of course, anything that involves cutting and gluing things. In the course of mastering these skills, children are also learning a variety of ways to communicate and express themselves—something experts feel is important to developing emotional intelligence. Along the way, some children will discover and develop real talents and lifelong interests. A playroom may not seem like a serious enough place for such important things, but, after all, play is the work of the child.

As big as the ones used at school but a lot cuter, this practical chalkboard, bulletin board, and art paper dispenser encourage creativity and communication. The easy-care floor stands up to coloring messes and offers plenty of space to play.

Colorful painted wood screens are solid below, airy above to offer a measure of privacy without blocking access to light and air. A kid-size table is decorated with bright-hued geometric shapes that echo the design on the screens.

229

Ocean Adventures

Many children's baths have fish, boats, or the sea as a motif, but few are as exciting as this little charmer. A glorious aquamarine blue plus splashy white creates a lively background for an ocean-inspired bath. Against these fresh-air hues, bold red, royal, and yellow accents stand out like racing flags. Cabana stripes on the tub are just one example of this spirited vision. The owners' collection of vacation souvenirs, including wooden ships, natural shells, carved seagulls, ocean creatures, and lots more adorn the room. They're especially striking in an ambitious collage on the wall above the tub. If you or your child have accumulated this type of memorabilia but don't know how to display it to advantage, why not show it all off where your child can enjoy it every day?

Colorful and casual, a collage assembled from miniature boats, shells, and assorted rustic souvenirs is a fun work of art that also has personal meaning for the room's young user. The display is tall, but the shelf it rests on is very narrow so it doesn't get in a bather's way.

Rustic little sailboats make a flotilla of fun along a white-painted alcove wall. Other types of collectibles would work just as well, as long as they don't have sharp points or protrude too far from the wall and as long as they can tolerate the high moisture levels in a bath.

A deep window alcove scoops in maximum sunlight when painted bright white. Clever recessed and wall-hung display shelves in aqua and yellow let accessories really stand out.

In the Fun Zone

Storage is a big challenge in any child's room. As parents and teachers know, kids aren't naturally neat, but they won't play with toys that are all in a jumble. That's understandable—you know how daunting a cleanup chore such as spring cleaning the garage can feel, and you're a grown-up! For kids, it's just plain overwhelming. To help children keep their books and playthings visible, accessible, and orderly, the right storage pieces can make a real difference. In the areas shown here, study areas and active play zones are set up for youngsters' convenience. Shelves are shallow, drawers are ample, and there's plenty of room to move around. A color scheme of bright white and primary hues boosts visibility and excitement.

A writing desk and computer desk sometimes seem at odds, but this clever unit makes plenty of separate but equal room for both. In between the two workstations, a dollhouse-inspired bookshelf stashes a library in style.

Primary colors seem tailor-made for kids in the primary grades. Brightly hued cubbyhole storage and an energizing red desk work well against the graphic on the wall. Designer: Susan Huckvale Arann, ASID, American & International Design.

A generously scaled wall unit combines conventional bookshelves with school-style cubbyhole storage. Deep bins and drawers create a niche that includes a cozy bench and a blackboard/drawing board. Designer: Tamara Harmon, CID, T.H. Designs, Inc.

233

Attic Hideaways

Children love to squirrel themselves away in little nests of their own. It's an instinct that can come in handy when the best space you have for a playroom is under the eaves. These adorable spaces may have low ceilings, but they've also got high aspirations. Instead of fighting the rooms' quirky shapes, the decor plays up the romance of it all. If you don't have relatively large pretty windows, maximize whatever natural light your attic room gets with bright white paint on the window frames. Walls painted or papered in pale tints are also important to capture maximum light, but you can embellish the look with airy prints or murals. Furnish with small-scale heirlooms or whimsical resale shop finds, and you've got a playroom even a grownup would love!

Like a Monet painting come to life, a painted garden walk gives this attic floor a whole new dimension. Old-fashioned perennials climb the walls for the look of a secret garden. Victorian-style wicker furnishings have a timeless appeal. Designer: Norma Hayman Interior Design.

A tiny space is full of garden-inspired delights, including a pink and green color scheme and a lattice motif along the walls and flowering trompe l'oeil branches. Piles of ruffled pillows in easy-care cotton are wonderfully inviting.

Prim and timeless documentary-print wallpaper lends an airy look to this room, but the traditional furniture looks downright funky with whimsical carrot legs. A big cozy chair is just right for a cuddle and a story. Pretty rope molding gives a finished look to built-in storage shelves. Designer: Delia Spradley, Spradley Interiors. Stylist: Joetta Moulden.

Light and Lively

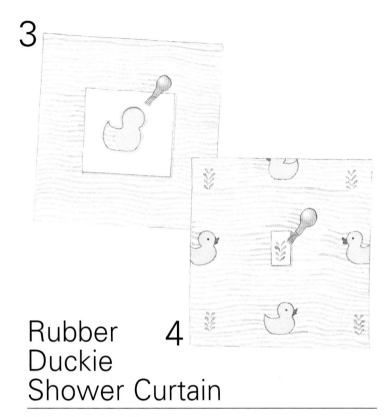

3

4

Rubber Duckie Shower Curtain

Although repainting the walls is usually the easiest, most economical way to change the look of a room, that's not always true when much of a room is tiled. If your child's bathroom tiles are in reasonably good shape, you can add color and pattern to them with stick-ons or you can stencil small designs at random using china paints. Then, extend the look with more stenciled designs on the shower curtain, toothbrush holder, step stool, towels—whatever. If you don't want to get too carried away with repeating a pattern, look for a related pattern; for example, if you're using mostly flowers, throw in a butterfly here or there. Repeat a color note in several spots around the room for a charming coordinated look that's fresh and easy.

What You'll Need
Fabric shower curtain
Tape measure
Painter's tape
Fabric medium
Acrylic paint
Stencil spray adhesive
1-inch stencil brush
⅜-inch stencil brushes, 3
Soft, clean cloth
Iron and ironing board

1. Prewash and dry curtain according to manufacturer's instructions.

2. Purchase rubber duckie and water splash stencils or make your own out of clear plastic (see page 62). To plan out design on shower curtain, leave approximately 14

inches between ducks horizontally and vertically. Place small piece of tape at these locations.

3. Follow manufacturer's instructions to add fabric medium to paint. Center duck stencil on piece of tape from step 2; remove tape. Stencil yellow with 1-inch brush. Repeat at every tape mark, flipping stencil over a few times for visual interest. Stencil eyes and feathers gray and beak orange with ⅜-inch brushes. Repeat on all ducks.

4. With blue paint and water splash stencil, add water around each duck and between every 2 ducks, both horizontally and vertically. Let dry. Place clean cloth over design, and run iron over cloth to heat-set paint.

Do your plain white tiles look clean but a bit bland? Liven them up with tile accents that are self-adhesive, washable, removable, and reusable as well as water-resistant. You could also use ceramic/china paints found in craft stores. Manufacturer: Blonder Wallcoverings.

Rubber duckies stenciled onto a shower curtain repeat the bright yellow note from the sunny walls. Special paints you can use on china, washable fabrics, and other surfaces let you carry a motif throughout the room. Stencil artist: Chris Bjorkeson, Stencil Planet.

Alive with Color

Rich and bold, the hues used in this spacious playroom look just right, thanks to the use of some basic color how-tos. While all the hues are intense, the ones used in abundance on the floor and walls are cool so they don't overwhelm. Against this deep sea of emerald green and royal blue, accents in warm yellow and red stand out in just the right proportion. They're energizing but not overheated. Using lots of white on the ceiling provides visual relief from the bold hues. (Studies show most people are more comfortable in a room that's dark on the lower part, light on the top, to mimic the earth and sky.) Bright white around the windows maximizes the room's intake of light, further enhancing the feeling of balance. Most of a child's responses to color proportions won't be at a conscious level, but they'll enjoy spending time in a room that feels both exciting and comfortable.

Color striping gives simple furniture pieces like this toy chest a refreshing new look. A few hours of effort and you've got a nearly instant heirloom. Paint also helps protect the wood below, extending its life. Just be sure the paints you use are child-safe.

You don't need expensive furniture or elaborate wall treatments to put together a play space kids will love. Just choose simple sturdy pieces from a resale shop or an unfinished furniture store, and treat them to lusciously intense colors. Stylist: Amy Leonard. Manufacturer: The Glidden Company.

Just Hangin' Out

Everything a youngster could wish for is taken care of in this up-to-the-minute play/study room. When a space is this thoughtfully put together, homework feels almost like play.

Kids are naturally forward-looking, but they also crave cozy reassurance. This play/study room delivers both innovation and comfort. Futuristic furniture delights the eye, while warm colors and traditional surfaces provide the necessary grounding. The room is not only appealing to kids, but it's also a winner with those who love them. Here's where the children can do their homework, play computer games, and read to Grandma or have her read to them. The to-scale ice cream parlor mural is a masterpiece of trompe l'oeil, while a vintage Coke machine and full-size popcorn cart provide real snacks. Furniture has rounded corners in case all that floor space inspires some impromptu roughhousing. Designed for kids, this is a room the whole family can love.

Rich colors and a pattern inspired by Matisse cutouts give this cozy upholstered seating great eye appeal. All the furniture is very modern, but curvy lines and smooth corners soften the look in a delightful way. Designer: Carol Spong, ASID; Carol Spong, ASID Interior Design.

Colorful pint-size bath fixtures are almost as cute as your little one. The Lilliputian look is elegantly vintage, with a giggle. Deep, rich colored walls set off the fixtures' lighter hues. Choose fixtures you can replace with conventional-size pieces later; store the heirloom mini fixtures for the next generation. Manufacturer: Chamber Tots.

Miniature Marvels

At one time, a bath designed just for children was a novel idea, but, today, many homes have a bath reserved just for the family's children. The next step in kid-size luxury may be bath fixtures that are sized for youngsters. Instead of step stools to reach the sink and plastic contraptions to make the toilet seat fit a child better, a suite of fixtures actually designed for young children is safer and more comfortable. Choose a system with a sink and tub that have antiscald devices and one in which all fixtures have conventionally sized plumbing so you can switch them out when your kids get bigger. In a supremely kid-friendly bath like this, the only thing that remains the same as in a conventional bath is the ironclad rule: Never leave a child in the tub unattended for even a moment.

A bath of his own is a luxury, but a bath filled with fixtures sized for a preschooler is a dream come true. This nostalgic bath is comfortable and fun for a lucky little one, and its Victorian dollhouse charm will beguile indulgent parents. Manufacturer: Chamber Tots.

Magical Impressions

The most delightful thing about decorating a child's room is that you can let your own imagination run free. You don't have to worry about whether teddy bears and butterflies go together or if you dare use a chest of drawers that looks like a person-size carrot. Your child will be happy to help you come up with wacky and wonderful images that can come to life with today's nontraditional wallcoverings, borders, furnishings, and decorative accents galore. If you're tired of the usual color schemes, try hot tropical pastels, jewel tones, or cotton candy tints. As long as you repeat some of your basic colors in at least three places in the room, you can mix them up with abandon and the room will still look nicely planned—not haphazard.

Young children love the game of popping blocks (or any small toys) into holes, as parents often learn to their dismay. This clever storage unit makes it fun to put little toys away through the small windows in the cupboard doors. A daybed piled with pillows is a simple charmer.

Soft orange, deep purple, mint green and red, blue, and yellow? Sounds garish, but, thanks to wallcoverings that contain all these hues, everything comes together with verve and harmony. Manufacturer: Brewster Wallcovering Company.

An armoire of simple pine is a visual treat with its over-the-top jigsawed contours. It's a perfect companion to a wacky carrot that's really a small chest of drawers. Custom painting makes each piece into art furniture. Manufacturer: Posh Tots.

Daytime Drama

Whether your children play in the latest "bonus room" or a tried-and-true basement recreation room, you want to give them a space that really works for them. The best way to plan a room this size is to zone it by activity. You'll need a hard surface for active or messy play; a soft surface for general roughhousing and TV watching; a table (or two) for projects, homework, and snacking; a desk for computer use; and easy-to-use storage for books, toys, videos, and more. Be sure to include some furniture that's scaled for adults, too—especially a comfortable chair where you can all cuddle up for storytime. A hefty dash of black adds a sense of sophisticated drama to the fun.

Bold graphic treatments give this dramatic room an extra jolt of excitement. You can get away with dark walls when the ceilings are extra high and tall windows scoop in the light. Lots of strategically placed artificial lighting is also used to spotlight work and play areas both day and night. Designer: Barbara Ostrom Associates.

For an artistic youngster, a corner devoted to painting is a rewarding idea. This smartly designed area features easy-care hard-surface flooring and a kid-size easel plus a unit to store and dispense rolls of drawing paper and other craft tools. Nearby, a sink and tier of cubbyhole storage units make everyday cleanup easier. Designer: Lee Najman Design.

Fun and Functional

Your child's bedroom isn't the only place where fun, safe, cleverly designed furnishings are important. Playrooms are a great place for whimsical furniture, pieces designed to facilitate craft projects and homework, and other special accents that reflect your child's personal interests. Bathrooms may be mostly installed fixtures and fittings, but that doesn't mean you can't indulge in some child-inspired pieces. Clever, colorful, and whimsical furnishings are available from manufacturers who've made a science out of understanding what kids need and like. You'll want to choose with an eye to safety and function first, of course. After that, feel free to indulge in the looks that will bring a smile, even when it's time to do homework or brush teeth.

Investment furniture for kids doesn't have to be stuffy. This grandfather clock takes classic design concepts and gives them a playful twist that's wonderfully timely. Beautiful crafting means this whimsical heirloom will be going strong, from the toddler years through the teens and beyond. Manufacturer: Straight Line Designs Inc.

It's never too early to help children appreciate good design and the grace of natural materials. Beautiful smooth-grain wood adds tactile and visual appeal to a playroom table with stools that double as storage bins. Designer: Alla Kazovsky. Manufacturer: Kids' Studio.

Sometimes you need heavy-duty permanent storage, and sometimes you just need a little extra help stashing things. Clever colorful bins in a variety of sizes are made of lightweight mesh so they're easy even for little ones to tote around. Just as important, they fold up when not in use. Retailer: The Container Store.

If your kids really love a certain story or image, why not keep it permanently in view? Wallcoverings and accent furnishings are popular choices, but even utilitarian fixtures can add to the fun. Here, a sink bowl becomes the canvas for a timeless nursery rhyme favorite come colorfully to life. Manufacturer: American Standard Inc.

Encourage kids' talent with an easel that's a work of art in itself. Height-adjustable for kids of all ages, the shatterproof white plastic structure holds work surfaces of clear acrylic and marker board. Circular cutouts store rolled artwork or drawing paper rolls, and translucent colored acrylic trays keep supplies in order. Designer: Alla Kazovsky. Manufacturer: Kids' Studio.

A little bit retro, a little bit classic, a whole lot of fun: A tepee this cute will be a favorite of boys and girls of all ages. Like their Old West prototypes, the tepee and coordinating camp stool are quickly folded and easily portable. Manufacturer: The Warm Biscuit Bedding Co.

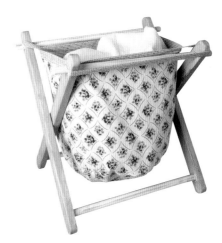

Colorful cotton towels, free of scratchy appliqués and fussy trims, are a must in a child's bath. For a special touch that makes even simple solid-color towels into stars, order them monogrammed with your child's name. Retailer: Garnet Hill.

Towels or clothes are less likely to end up on the bathroom floor when kids can toss them into a pretty little hamper like this one. The needlepoint-style rosebud print is a traditional charmer she'll be pleased to use. Manufacturer: The Warm Biscuit Bedding Co.

Resource Directory

ARCHITECTS & BUILDERS

DelValle Homes
1809 Central Avenue D
Ceres, California 95307-1806
phone 209-524-6885
Scott Meyers
(138, 139)

Tom Price
210 East Gore Street
Orlando, Florida 32806
phone 407-422-4422
(198)

Ray Kinner Builders
Los Angeles, California
phone 310-476-1824
Debra Jones (designer)
(188, 189)

Shope Reno Wharton
18 West Putnam Avenue
Greenwich, Connecticut 06830
phone 203-869-7250
fax 203-869-2804
(190)

ARTISTS, DECORATORS, DESIGNERS & STYLISTS

A Design Shoppe
1512 North Naperville Boulevard
Suite 152
Naperville, Illinois 60563
phone 630-245-0500
fax 630-245-0501
adesignshoppe@bigplanet.com
a-design-shoppe.com
Betty J. Weir
(58)

Adeeni Associates
940 Leavenworth Street, Number One
San Francisco, California 94109
phone 415-928-4685
adeeni@mindspring.com
Claudia Adetuyi
(85)

American & International Design
Staten Island, New York
Susan Huckvale Arann, ASID
(233)

Barbara Ostrom Associates
One International Boulevard
Mahwah, New Jersey 07495
phone 201-529-0444
(246)

Benner Interiors
223 Ronan Way
Neshanic Station, New Jersey 08853
phone 908-369-0098
bennerinteriors@msn.com
Jeanne Benner
(50)

Blailock Design
5120 Woodway, Suite 8009
Houston, Texas 77056
phone 713-513-2925
fax 713-961-3066
morton@hal-pc.org
Julia Blailock, ASID
(4–5, 102, 103)

Brockworks, Inc.
102 Ridgeway Court
Moneta, Virginia 24121
phone 540-297-8986
Whitney Brock
(92, 93)

Carol Spong, ASID Interior Design
P.O. Box 910575
San Diego, California 92121
phone 858-453-1700
fax 858-453-8360
Carol Spong, ASID
(228, 240, 241)

Design Sense
P.O. Box 4341
Rocky Mount, North Carolina 27804
phone 252-407-7772
lmphillipsnc@msn.com
Lynda M. Phillips
(6)

Diane Boyer Interiors
A Division of Bill Behrle Associates
271 Grove Avenue
Verona, New Jersey 07044
phone 973-239-4900
dboyer@behrlegroup.com
www.dianeboyer.com
Diane Boyer, ASID
(176, 177)

EJR Architects
phone 516-922-2479
Ellen Roche
(94, 95, 128, 129, 130, 131)

Steven Hammel
phone 212-995-5276
(94, 95, 128, 129, 130, 131)

Sunday Hendrickson
phone 310-440-9338
(166, 167, 194)

Spradley Interiors
1100 Cowards Creek Drive
Friendswood, Texas 77546
phone 281-996-5462
Delia Spradley
(162, 163, 168, 169)

Stencil Planet
P.O. Box 90
Berkeley Heights,
New Jersey 07922
phone 908-771-8967
fax 908-771-8910
www.stencilplanet.com
info@stencilplanet.com
Chris Bjorkeson
(237)

Stevens & Smith Designs
65 East Ridgewood Avenue
Ridgewood, New Jersey 07450
phone 201-670-6744

Susann Kelly Interiors
131 East 69th Street
New York, New York 10021
phone 212-988-7721
(116)

Suzanne Curtis Interior Design
11 Van Dyke Drive
Ho Ho Kus, New Jersey 07423
phone 201-670-9368
SCurtis@ASID@aol.com
Suzanne S. Curtis, ASID
(132, 133)

T.H. Designs Inc.
464 Pacific Avenue
Pacifica, California 94044
phone 650-359-6851
fax 650-359-4010
(232, 233)

Cyndi Tuma
Newport Beach, California
phone 310-440-9338
(166, 167)

Mark Wilkinson
Overton House
High Street Bromham
Nr. Chippenham UNITED KINGDOM
phone 011-44-1380-850184
fax 011-44-1380-850184
rjackson@mwf.com
(contents, 106, 107, 110, 111, 118, 119,
124, 125, 136, 137)

RETAILERS
Bombay Kids
P.O. Box 161009
Fort Worth, Texas 76161-9967
phone 800-829-7789
www.bombaykids.com
(contents, 143, 156, 157, 178, 179, 181,
182, 183, 208, 209)

The Container Store
2000 Valwood Parkway
Dallas, Texas 75234
phone 800-786-7315
www.containerstore.com
(179, 215, 248)

Garnet Hill
231 Main Street
Franconia, New Hampshire 03580
phone 800-622-6216
fax 888-842-9696
www.garnethill.com
(220, 221, 249)

Gautier USA, Inc.
3155 North Andrews Avenue Extension
Pompano Beach, Florida 33064
phone 954-975-3303
fax 954-975-3359
(30, 34, 45, 55, 181, 192, 193, 202, 203,
210, 211, 215)

JCPMedia L.P.
Atlanta, Georgia 30390-0100
phone 800-222-6161
fax 800-711-9485
www.JCPenney.com
(43, 200, 214, 215)

Lauren Alexandra
322 West 63rd Street
Kansas City, Missouri 64113
phone 816-822-2539
fax 816-822-8535
www.laurenalexandra.com
Pamela DiCapo (designer)
(69, 76, 82, 83, 96, 97, 100, 108, 109,
122, 123)

The Magic Moon
1900 Preston Road, Suite 269
Plano, Texas 75093
phone 888-333-1417
fax 972-612-2058
info@themagicmoon.com
www.themagicmoon.com
(68, 84, 101, 117, 207)

Room & Board
4600 North Memorial Highway
Minneapolis, Minnesota 55422
phone 763-588-7525
(105)

Spiegel Catalog, Inc.
P.O. Box 9209
Hampton, Virginia 23670-9998
phone 800-345-4500
fax 800-422-6697
www.spiegel.com
(179, 214)

MANUFACTURERS
3M
phone 888-364-3577
www.commandadhesive.com
(33, 187)

American Standard Inc.
One Centennial Avenue
P.O. Box 6820
Piscataway, New Jersey 08855-6820
phone 732-980-3000
fax 732-980-3335
(249)

Blonder Wallcoverings
phone 800-321-4070
www.blonderwall.com
(60, 217, 237)

Bratt Decor, Inc.
1103 North Washington Street
Baltimore, Maryland 21213
phone 888-24-BRATT
fax 410-327-4446
brattdecor.com
(105)

Brewster Wallcovering Co.
67 Pacella Park Drive
Randolph, Massachusetts 02368
phone 800-958-9580
www.brewsterwallcovering.com
(front cover, 9, 66–67, 116, 245)

Carey More Designs
4191 Carpinteria Avenue, Number Six
Carpinteria, California 93013
phone 805-566-9950
fax 805-566-2121
carey@careymoredesigns.com
careymoredesigns.com
(142)

Chamber Tots
The Old Bank, 36 High Street
Llanfyllin, Powys, Wales
ENGLAND 5Y22 5AQ
phone 01691649055
www.chambertots.co.uk
(242, 243)

Chic Shack
77 Lower Richmond Road
London, ENGLAND SW15 1ET
phone 0044-208-7857777
fax 0044-208-7890444
info@chicshack.net
www.chicshack.net
Maria Myers (designer)
(21, 23)

EG Furniture
381 Principal C.P. 294
La Pérade, Québec CANADA G0X 2J0
phone 888-422-5534
fax 888-329-8634
eg@egfurniture.com
www.egfurniture.com
(85, 205)

The Glidden Company
800-GLIDDEN
www.gliddenpaint.com
*Amy Leonard (stylist), Monica Buck
(photographer)*
(28, 80, 81, 172, 173, 238, 239)

Grange
2 Henry Adams, Number 160
San Francisco, California 94103
(70, 71)

IMG
phone 415-292-5600
(70, 71)

Jane Keltner Designs, Inc.
94 Cumberland Boulevard
Memphis, Tennessee 38112
phone 800-487-8033
fax 901-458-0804
www.janekeltner.com
(104)

Forrest Jones
3274 Sacramento Street
San Francisco, California 94115
phone 415-567-2483
(70, 71)

Kids' Studio
8342 West Fourth Street
Los Angeles, California 90048
phone 323-655-4028
fax 323-655-4178
Alla Kazovsky (designer)
(12, 152, 153, 248, 249)

L&G Decorators
134 Route 46
Netcong, New Jersey 07857
phone 973-347-0305
(176, 177)

Lilypads
411 Perry Street
Springfield, Oregon 97477
phone 541-726-1879
www.home.earthlink.net/~lilypads
Diana Cuyler (designer)
(143)

Motif Designs
20 Jones Street
New Rochelle, New York 10802
phone 800-431-2424
Lyn Peterson (designer)
(38)

PJ Kids
306 Alexander Street
Princeton, New Jersey 08540
phone 609-683-5438
fax 609-683-8070
www.pjkids.com
(27, 47, 105, 143, 145, 170, 171)

Posh Tots
4501 Highwoods Parkway, Suite 200
Glen Allen, Virginia 23060
phone 866.POSHTOT
info@poshtots.com
www.poshtots.com
(245)

Schumacher
101 Henry Adams
San Francisco, California 94103
phone 415-621-7700
(70, 71)

Smellybottoms.com
41 King Street Hikurangi
Northland, NEW ZEALAND
phone 0064-9-4337440
www.smellybottoms.com
Meg O'Halloran (designer)
(143)

Stanley Furniture Co.
1641 Fairystone Park Highway
P.O. Box 30
Stanleytown, Virginia 24168
phone 276-627-2000
fax 276-269-4085
rcampbell@stanleyfurniture.com
www.stanleyfurniture.com
(186, 201, 206)

Straight Line Designs Inc.
1000 Parker Street
Vancouver, British Columbia
CANADA V6A 2H2
phone 604-251-9669
fax 604-251-1676
(142, 248)

Vermont Precision
249 Professional Drive
Morrisville, Vermont 05661
www.vermontprecisionwoodworks.com
(70, 71)

**Village, a Brand of
FSC Wallcoverings**
79 Madison Avenue
New York, New York 10016
phone 212-213-7860
fax 212-213-7640
www.fschumacher.com
(14, 41)

The Warm Biscuit Bedding Co.
139 Fulton Street, Suite 201
New York, New York 10038
phone 800-231-4231
fax 212-619-7294
www.warmbiscuit.com
(105, 150, 204, 249)

**Waverly, a Brand of
FSC Wallcoverings**
79 Madison Avenue
New York, New York 10016
phone 212-213-7860
fax 212-213-7640
www.fschumacher.com
(44, 48, 101)

PHOTOGRAPHERS
Abode Interiors Picture Library
Albion Court, One Pierce Street
Macclesfield, Cheshire
ENGLAND SK11 6ER
phone 011-44-1625-500-070
fax 011-44-1625-500-910
(back cover, contents, 29, 37, 46, 114,
115, 146, 147, 183, 204, 212, 213, 216,
218, 219)

Andrew McKinney Photography
180½ Tenth Avenue
San Francisco, California 94118
phone 415-752-4070
(70, 71)

Beateworks Inc.
2400 South Shenandoah Street
Los Angeles, California 90034
phone 310-558-1100
fax 310-842-8889
www.beateworks.com
(187)

Tom Bonner
1201 Abbot Kinney Boulevard
Venice, California 90291
phone 310-396-7125
tsbphoto@aol.com

Brad Simmons Photography
870 Craintown Road
Perryville, Kentucky 40468
phone 859-332-8400
fax 859-332-4433
www.bradsimmons.com
(20, 25, 63, 145, 151, 162, 163, 168, 169,
226, 227, 235)

D. Randolph Foulds Photography
12700 Triple Crown Road
North Potomac, Maryland 20878
phone 301-948-7048
fax 301- 670-0268
foto-r@comcast.net
www.fouldsphoto.com
(144, 154, 155)

Dawn A. Merriman Photography
282 Bingham Court Northwest
Comstock Park, Michigan 49321
phone 616-785-1069
jdmerriman@attbi.com
(65)

Michael Dunne
54 Stoken Church Street
London, ENGLAND SW6 3TR
phone 011-44-207-736-6171
(191)

Jack Elka
P.O. Box 582
Anna Maria, Florida 34216
phone 941-778-2711
fax 941-778-3341
jack@jackelka.com
jackelka.com
(232)

Alain Giguère
288 rue Notre Dame Est
Victoriaville, Québec CANADA G6P 4A3
phone 819-758-8748
fax 819-758-9375
(85, 205)

Greg Page Photography
2800 Lyndale Avenue South
Minneapolis, Minnesota 55408
phone 612-874-0566
fax 612-874-8109
pagegi@aol.com
(164, 165)

Hickey-Robertson
1419 Branard Street
Houston, Texas 77006
phone 713-522-7258
(4–5, 102, 103)

The Interior Archive Ltd.
Six Colville Mews
Lonsdale Road
London, ENGLAND W11 2DA
phone 020-7221-9922
fax 020-7221-9933
Fritz von der Schulenburg, Edina van der Wyck
(16–17, 53, 112, 113, 158, 159, 229, 230, 231)

Jay Rosenblatt Photography
P.O. Box 103
Milburn, New Jersey 07041
jayrose2@earthlink.net
www.jayrosenblatt.com
(176, 177)

Ken Vaughan Photographer
2010 Glenwick
Garland, Texas 75040
phone 972-414-0118
(101, 207

Dennis Krukowski
329 East 92 Street, Suite 1D
New York, New York 10128
phone 212-860-0912
fax 212-860-0913
(contents, 88, 89, 224, 225, 234)

Raymond Lee
6404 Lock Raven Boulevard
Baltimore, Maryland 21239
phone 410-323-5764
(105)

Mark Lohman Photography
1021 South Fairfax Avenue
Los Angeles, California 90019
phone 323-933-3359
Mark Lohman, Janet Lohman (designer)
(15, 74, 75, 126, 127, 194, 140, 141, 160, 161, 166, 180, 184, 185, 188, 189, 194, 222, 223)

Melabee M. Miller Photography
29 Beechwood Place
Hillside, New Jersey 07205
phone 908-527-9121
fax 908-527-0242
(132, 133, 234)

Adrian Mendoza
1325 H Street
Modesto, California 95355
phone 209-578-2222
mdunbar@modbee.com
(138, 139)

Bradley Olman
P.O. Box 2157
Red Bank, New Jersey 07701
phone 800-407-5680 or 732-450-2050
olmanphoto@aol.com
(50, 120, 121)

Phillip Ennis Photography
114 Millertown Road
Bedford, New York 10506
phone 914-234-9574
www.phillip-ennis.com
(22, 52, 72, 73, 78, 79, 116, 195, 198, 244, 246)

Marc Angelo Ramos
30 Kingston
San Francisco, California 94110
phone 415-336-7517
fax 415-824-4813
repetitiveculture@earthlink.net
pivotculture.com
(85)

Samu Studios
11 PD Harris Road
Saratoga Springs, New York 12866
phone 518-581-7026
(69, 90, 91, 94, 95, 98, 99, 107, 128, 129, 130, 131, 134, 135, 247)

Shenkin Photography
330 East Roosevelt Road
Lombard, Illinois 60148
phone 630-935-5055
(58)

Stacey Brandford Photography
Nine Davies Avenue, Studio 103
Toronto, Ontario CANADA M4M 2A6
phone 416-463-8877
fax 416-461-8705
www.staceybrandford.com
(196, 197)

Tim Street-Porter
2704 Watsonia Terrace
Los Angeles, California 90068
phone 323-874-4278
(10, 18, 26, 229, 233)

Laurence Taylor
2000-B Alden Road
Orlando, Florida 32803
phone 407-897-2005
(7, 198)

Thompson Martin Photography
108 Garfield Avenue
London, Ontario CANADA N6C 2B6
phone 519-679-5597
thompsonmartin@sympatio.ca
www.thompsonmartin.biz
Steven Martin
(174, 175)

Travis Manning Photography
PO Box 2474
Roanoke, Virginia 24010
phone 540-819-8014
tsmanning@hotmail.com
(contents, 92, 93, 148, 149)

Photo Credits

Front cover: **Brewster Wallcovering Co.**

Back cover: **Abode Interior Picture Library**

3M: 33, 187 (top); **Abode Interior Picture Library:** contents, 29, 37, 46, 114, 115, 146, 147, 183 (right center), 204 (top), 212, 213, 216, 218, 219; **Adeeni Associates/Marc Angelo Ramos:** 85 (top); **Lauren Alexandra/Bill Matthews:** 69 (top), 76, 82, 83, 96, 97, 100, 108, 109, 122, 123; **American Standard Inc.:** 249 (top left); **Beateworks Inc./Scotto/Inside:** 187 (bottom); **Benner Interiors/Bradley Olman:** 50; **Blailock Design/Hickey-Robertson:** 4–5, 102, 103; **Blonder Wallcoverings:** 60, 217, 237; **Bombay Kids:** contents, 143, 156, 157, 178, 179 (top left & bottom left), 181, 182, 183 (top & left center), 208, 209; **Brad Simmons Photography:** 20, 25, 63, 145 (bottom), 151, 162, 163, 168, 169, 226, 227, 235; **Bratt Decor, Inc./Raymond Lee:** 105 (bottom right); **Brewster Wallcovering Co.:** 66–67; Can You Imagine? Collection: 245 (top); Jack & Jill IX Collection: 9, 116 (top); **Carey More Designs:** 142; **Carol Spong, ASID Interior Design/Brady Architectural Photography:** 228, 240, 241; **Karen Cashman/Perspectives/David Van Scott Photography:** 40, 76; **Chamber Tots:** 242, 243; **Chic Shack/Jon Bouchier:** 21, 23; **The Container Store:** 179 (bottom right), 215 (top left & bottom right), 248 (bottom right); **Design Sense/Lynda M. Phillips:** 6; **A Design Shoppe/Shenkin Photography:** 58; **Diane Boyer Interiors/Jay Rosenblatt Photography:** 176, 177; **EG Furniture/Alain Giguère:** 85 (bottom), 205; **Garnet Hill:** 220, 221, 249 (center); **Gautier USA, Inc.:** 30, 34, 45, 55, 181, 192, 193, 202, 203, 210, 211, 215 (bottom left); **The Glidden Company:** 28, 80, 81, 172, 173, 238, 239; **Holdren's Interiors, Inc./Travis Manning Photography:** contents, 92, 93, 148, 149; **The Interior Archive, Ltd.:** Fritz van der Schulenburg: 16–17, 53, 158, 159, 229 (bottom), 230, 231; Edina van der Wyck: 112, 113; **INTERIORS by Decorating Den:** D. Randolph Foulds Photography: 144, 154, 155; Dawn A. Merriman Photography: 65; Greg Page Photography: 164, 165; Steven Martin/Thompson Martin Photography: 174, 175; Bradley Olman: 120, 121; Stacey Brandford Photography: 196, 197; **J. Haidlen Design Associates/Adrian Mendoza:** 138, 139; **JCPMedia L.P.:** 43, 200, 214 (bottom left & bottom right), 215 (top right); **Jane Keltner Designs, Inc.:** 104; **Jennifer Norris Interiors:** 86, 87; **Karen Graham Interiors/Andrew McKinney Photography:** 70, 71; **Kids' Studio/Tom Bonner:** 12, 152, 153, 248 (bottom left), 249 (top right); **©Dennis Krukowski:** contents, 88, 89, 224, 225, 234 (bottom); **Laura Bohn Design Associates/Michael Dunne:** 191; **Lilypads/Diana Cuyler:** 143; **The Magic Moon:** Henry Biber Photography: 68, 84, 117, 207 (bottom); Ken Vaughan Photographer: 101 (left), 207 (top); **Mark Lohman Photography:** 15, 74, 75, 126, 127, 140, 141, 160, 161, 166, 180, 184, 185, 188, 189, 194, 222, 223; **Melabee M. Miller Photography:** 132, 133, 234 (top); **Mojo Stumer Associates, p.c.:** 8; **Montanna & Associates/Laurence Taylor:** 7, 198 (top); **Motif Designs:** 38; **Phillip Ennis Photography:** 22, 52, 72, 73, 78, 79, 116 (bottom), 195, 198 (bottom), 244, 246; **PJ Kids:** 27, 47, 105 (bottom left), 143, 145 (top), 170, 171; **Posh Tots:** 245 (bottom); **Room & Board:** 105 (top left); **Samu Studios:** 69 (bottom), 90, 94, 95, 98, 99, 107 (top), 128, 131, 134, 135, 247; Photo by Mark Samu Courtesy Hearst Magazines: 90, 91, 95, 129, 130; **Smellybottoms.com:** 143; **Spiegel Catalog, Inc.:** 179, 214 (top); **Stanley Furniture Co.:** 186, 201, 206; **Straight Line Designs Inc.:** 142, 248 (top); **Tim Street-Porter:** 10, 18, 26, 229 (top), 233; **T.H. Designs Inc./Jack Elka:** 232; **Village, a Brand of FSC Wallcoverings:** 14, 41; **The Warm Biscuit Bedding Co.:** 105 (top right), 249 (left center & right center); Jennifer Krough: 150, 204 (bottom); **Waverly, a Brand of FSC Wallcoverings:** 44, 48, 101 (right); **Mark Wilkinson:** contents, 106, 107 (bottom), 110, 111, 118, 119, 124, 125, 136, 137.